DATE DUE FOR RETURN

The
Nottinghamshire
Village Book

UNIVERSITY OF NOTTINGHAM

WITH

66 000

D0806520

FRO

Y

THE VILLAGES OF BRITAIN SERIES

Other counties in this series include:

Avon*
Bedfordshire*
Berkshire*
Buckinghamshire*
Cambridgeshire*
Dorset
Essex*
Gloucestershire*
Hampshire
Herefordshire*
Hertfordshire*
Kent
Leicestershire*
　& Rutland*
Middlesex*

Northamptonshire*
Oxfordshire
Powys Montgomery*
Shropshire*
Somerset*
Staffordshire*
Suffolk
Surrey
East Sussex
West Sussex
Warwickshire*
West Midlands*
Wiltshire
Worcestershire*

*Published in conjunction with County Federations of Women's Institutes.

The
Nottinghamshire
Village Book

Compiled by the Nottinghamshire
Federation of Women's Institutes from notes
and illustrations sent by Institutes in the County

Published jointly by
Countryside Books, Newbury
and the NFWI, Newark

First Published 1989
© Nottinghamshire Federation of Women's Institutes 1989

All rights reserved. No reproduction
permitted without the prior permission
of the publishers:

Countryside Books,
3 Catherine Road,
Newbury, Berkshire

ISBN 1 85306 057 7

Cover photograph of Car Colston
taken by Christine Barker
of Car Colston & Screveton WI

Produced through MRM Associates Ltd, Reading
Typeset by Acorn Bookwork, Salisbury
Printed in Great Britain by J.W. Arrowsmith Ltd, Bristol

00844

Foreword

Gem-shaped, in the heart of England, lies Nottinghamshire, a gem with many facets. In the south, lush, green pastureland and acres of mixed farming, including roses, encompass the historical city of Nottingham, home of Raleigh Cycles, Boots the Chemists, John Player Tobacco and, of course, the famous Nottingham lace and textile industries. To the west and north will be found the beautiful Sherwood Forest and an abundance of farmland, as well as the vast coalfields that inspired D. H. Lawrence.

There is so much to discover in this County of contrasts. The sails of a working windmill spin in the shadow of a chain of giant power stations, a modern Olympic-standard water sports centre lies adjacent to the meandering river Trent and high-tech farms operate in the same area as mediaeval strip farming.

As well as the legend of Robin Hood, Nottinghamshire is famous for Goose Fair and William Booth, founder of the Salvation Army; for the Luddites and the Pilgrim Fathers; for the Bramley Apple and the Battle of East Stoke.

I hope these brief paragraphs encourage you to read on and then to visit, because there is so much more, as you will find. The WI members who have contributed to this book have been enriched by the experience of researching the history of their villages and communities.

Echoing Blake's immortal words, Notts. certainly is a 'green and pleasant land'.

Jacky Toplis
County Chairman

Acknowledgements

The Nottinghamshire Federation of Women's Institutes wish to thank all those members, their families and friends who have worked so hard to research and provide information for this book and who have provided the excellent drawings.

Also a special thank you to Jenny Holmes, the co-ordinator for the project.

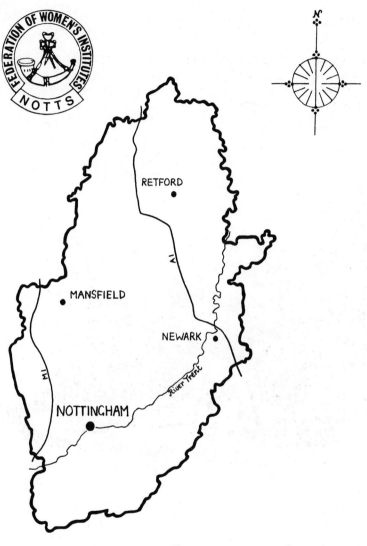

FEDERATION OF WOMEN'S INSTITUTES

NOTTS

N

RETFORD

A1

MANSFIELD

NEWARK

M1

River Trent

NOTTINGHAM

County of

NOTTINGHAMSHIRE

Plough Sunday at Tithby

Alverton ✍

This very small hamlet of only eight houses, lies either side of the Newark to Orston road. The old Staunton Church of England school is in this village but is now a private residence. It is said to be haunted by a teacher who was actually murdered at the school. Recent residents have reported being able to hear voices upstairs whilst sitting in the kitchen.

One of the larger houses, 'The Chestnuts', is also reputed to have a ghost. Two separate sightings both gave identical descriptions of an elderly lady in Victorian dress. This is thought to be Mary Brown, who gave up her job as a sewing maid to Queen Victoria, when her brother's wife died and moved into the house to become housekeeper to him and his four children, ruling with a 'rod of iron'. In later years when noises were heard upstairs it was noted that 'Aunty Polly was on the warpath again'.

The surrounding land is exclusively farmed and the village is said to be one of the smallest in Nottinghamshire.

Annesley ✍

Off the M1 motorway at junction 27 lie the villages of Annesley, Annesley Woodhouse, Kirkby Woodhouse, Nuncargate and Newstead, all once part of Sherwood Forest.

After leaving the motorway, heading for Mansfield, the first building on the right is Annesley Hall and the ruins of the church, the sole remains of the old Annesley village. In the graveyard the oldest dated gravestone is in the early 1700s.

In contrast, opposite and set back from the road is the recently established Kodak site, skirted by the very old osier beds and a pond famous locally for tadpoles. Also close by is a popular spinney where in the past 'conkers' for children were abundant.

The present Annesley church will appear in view on a hill to the right. Here one can turn and visit Newstead Colliery village, with its terraces of houses where miners lived, and follow a route through to Newstead Abbey, Lord Byron's home.

Annesley church is a recent building, the earlier one having been burnt down, it is thought, by the Suffragettes. It overlooks a panoramic scene of Hollinwell Golf Course, woods, fields and Annesley Colliery with its two long rows of houses known locally as 'The Rows'. It is said that there is no higher point than the top of the church spire until the Urals in Russia.

The Badger Box public house is a newish building replacing the original one, where the owner once kept a badger in the garden. On its death it was stuffed and placed in a box for all to see, hence the name.

Turning left to Annesley Woodhouse, a long gradual rise leads to the oldest part of the village. This consists of streets of terraced properties with old names such as Wesley Street, Sherwood Street, Fox Street and Reform Street. The latter housed the village bakery. There is a post office, two chapels (both of which have celebrated 100 years of witness), shops and a doctors' surgery. The cottages by the surgery were once part of the old malthouses, thus the nearby junction is known as the Malthouse Corner.

Directly ahead at Malthouse Corner is Salmon Lane. A house on the left used to be a blacksmith's forge. Its neighbour, surrounded by sycamores, belonged to another doctor who dispensed his own medicines. Further down the lane one can walk through Davies Bottoms and by its haunted house ruins. Further on is the Dumbles, a local beauty spot with a wealth of wild flowers.

Going right at Malthouse Corner, there is a detached house which was the first place of worship for the Methodists in the village. Three new detached houses next to this building stand on the site of an old stone cottage owned by a man called Booth Edison. He willed the interest from the sale of the property to provide prizes for the children at Annesley and Kirkby Woodhouse schools. This still continues today.

Two public houses stand close by, the General Havelock and the Forest Tavern, which have been part of the village for generations. The land between the two was once the site of a mill.

St John's church has no belfry, as the sandy soil on which it was built would not carry the weight of a belfry tower.

The road leads to Kirkby Woodhouse and an estate of council houses built in the 1950s covers an old greyhound track. This area has views of the M1 and Bentinck Colliery. Further round the road is an old Baptist chapel dated 1754, which was modernised in 1818 and again in 1866. The old Kirkby Woodhouse school, over 100 years old, is now a nursing home, with a modern school sited at the rear of it.

You now enter Nuncargate, flanked on the right with a wall of old mill stones, now sadly covered by cement. These stones came from Fryer's Mill, which stood in Mill Lane opposite the old primary school.

Nuncargate is famed for its cricketers, all local lads, the most noted giving their names to the House system of the school – Hardstaff, Larwood, Staples and Voce. All represented their county and country at cricket.

During the Second World War these villages were home to many evacuees and 'Bevin Boys', some of whom still keep in contact with their hosts. Other visitors were Italian prisoners of war who worked on farmland in the locality.

Although originally the villages made up a farming community, there were a few cottage industries, such as wheelwrights, framework knitters, blacksmiths and potters. As the pits opened in the 20th century mining became the predominant industry for the village men. Three collieries opened in this area.

Aslockton & Whatton ❧

The villages of Aslockton and Whatton lie on the edge of the beautiful Vale of Belvoir and are separated by the main Nottingham to Grantham railway line, the footpath making a very pleasant walk of about half a mile. Aslockton is the larger of the two villages and has the post office, the home-made bread shop and the butcher, whose family have served the villages for well over 150 years. 'Fine Ales' are also to be found at The Cranmer Arms and the Greyhound, the wall of which still boasts – albeit faintly – of having 'good stabling'.

Farming is part of the community, with sheep and cattle and the wonderful colour of the rape fields in the early summer. Most of the working population from both villages now commutes to Nottingham, but quite a number are employed at the Young Offenders Institute in Whatton.

The older children attend the comprehensive school at Bingham about three miles away. The village school is named after a famous inhabitant of the 15th century, Archbishop Thomas Cranmer, who spent his child-hood here before going to Cambridge University at the age of 14. He worshipped with his father, also named Thomas, in the 13th century church of St John of Beverley in Whatton, and one can well imagine them walking across the fields, listening to the bells pealing out to call everyone to church.

The present church of St Thomas in Aslockton was not built until the latter part of the 19th century.

Racehorses are part and parcel of the village scene as there are training stables nearby and stable lads are to be seen every day exercising the horses.

How far-sighted of the villagers, after their celebrations of the Jubilee of King George V, to start a fund for a village hall. The hall is still used regularly by a variety of clubs of all ages and is still regarded as one of the best halls in the area.

Attenborough

Because of its geographical position, enclosed by the bypass and the river Trent, Attenborough is a compact area which retains its village character though only seven miles from Nottingham, between Beeston and Long Eaton.

There is documented evidence of monks having lived near the church, and the ancient church door, dating back to medieval time and a 12th century tombstone have been re-hung in the porch. It is an interesting and well maintained church, clothed in history, including on display the christening records of Oliver Cromwell's granddaughter. His daughter was married to Colonel Ireton, who lived in the house adjoining the church.

The present Parish Clerk is the last in line of her family who have held that position for over 300 years.

In the churchyard is the communal grave of about 150 people killed in an explosion at nearby Chilwell Ordnance Depot in 1918.

For some years gravel has been extracted from the river bank and large lagoons have been formed from the workings. The area is now a well known and much visited nature reserve, a haven for wild life including foxes. Walkers, bird-watchers and anglers make good use of the banks, and boats from nearby sailing clubs are much in evidence on the river.

A field bought collectively is now the village green and provides playing areas for the successful football and cricket teams, and is a hive of activity for the Church Fete on the first Saturday in July.

Most children attend primary and secondary schools in nearby Chilwell, but there is a small preparatory school in the village. Recreational activities are provided by Beavers, Cubs, Scouts, Brownies and Guides. A tennis club has prospered for many years and more recently a bowls club has given more choice for the residents although there is evidence of the existence of a bowls club in 1909.

There are many attractive gardens, some of whose owners have formed a small Garden Club.

Averham 🦢

Averham lies between Newark and Southwell but is bypassed by the A617. The name was first recorded as Egrum, in later years became Averam, and whilst it is now called Averham, it is pronounced 'Airam'. Originally the village was situated by a small stream but is now centred around the crossroads of Staythorpe Road and the old main road.

In the 16th century the Sutton family were the local squires and in 1594 the small brook was insufficient for their needs, so a cut was made from the river Trent near Farndon to the brook. This created such a powerful current that the millers and inhabitants of Newark prosecuted the Suttons for taking their water and the family was ordered by the court to build a weir and maintain it. In the 17th century when Robert Sutton lived in a large manor house with a moat on Church Lane, Newark was surrendered to the Parliamentarians and he, being a Royalist, had his house burned to the ground.

The oldest road through the village would appear to be Church Lane, continuing across Staythorpe Lane and Pinfold Lane. Many of the old cottages are situated here, along with the rectory, remains of the manor house moat, the old forge, a strip of common land formerly known as the village green and the site of the old pound, now built on. Here also is the old communal 'bake oven'. Most of the cottages have similar roofs and chimneys and were probably built by the Sutton (later Manners-Sutton) estate.

The church of St Michael and All Angels is situated by the river. It was originally a wooden building, then superseded by a stone one which had later additions. It has Norman herringbone stones on one side. A porch was attached about 1500 with the initials on it of Thomas Sutton, 'who caused it to be built'. There are fierce gargoyles on church and porch. The tower has six bells. Inside there is a fine 15th century screen and two very fine Sutton monuments can be seen in the chancel. In 1984 vandals chopped off the hands of two recumbent figures and sprayed them with red paint but they have been excellently repaired. When doing so it was found that damage had been done to them before, probably by the Parliamentary forces during the Civil War. The altar was accidentally burned in 1978.

The rectory next to the church was built in 1839 but is now a nursing home for the elderly. In the rectory grounds is a unique private theatre called 'The Robin Hood Theatre'. It was built by the Rev Cyril Walker in 1912 and seats 150 people. Rev Walker, rector of the parish, had been a member of Oxford University Dramatic Society and was a friend of Sir Henry Irving and Bouchier. He started amateur theatricals in Averham. The productions were initially held in the village school. Among the company of actors at a later date was the Newark schoolboy, Donald Wolfit, later knighted for his services to the stage. More recently several famous actors have graced the stage of the theatre, which is now under the trusteeship of the Nottinghamshire County Council.

On Church Lane is the old dame school with teacher's house attached, which is now a private house. Here, children were taught reading, writing and 'summing', with needlework for the girls.

The old forge is situated on Staythorpe Road adjoining a house of a more recent date. This is believed to have been one of the coaching inns, along with Averill House, as this was the coach route from Newark to Southwell via Rolleston and Fiskerton. Close by are two old cottages which have now been made into one larger residence. Some stones for their original building were taken from the ruins of the manor house. Inside walls were made from straw and horse dung. The corner cottage was, for many years, the home of the Lee family – joiners and wheel-wrights.

Averham, Kelham and Staythorpe are now one parish. The residents have widely different occupations – farm workers, professional people, retired people and power station workers. Most of them travel to Newark and Staythorpe by car to their employment.

Balderton ✖

Travelling north from Grantham on the A1, Balderton is the village immediately before Newark on Trent, and the tollhouse is a reminder of the coach traffic which once used the Great North Road. In the last 80 years the village has expanded, from a rural one, centred on a main street with a medieval church and village inn, to a community of 9,700 people. A large manufacturing works, various small industries, shops and schools serve the new housing estates which extend onto what was once farmland, allotments and open space.

The crocketed spire of St Giles' church dominates the junction of Main

Street and the road which once carried travellers north and south between London and Edinburgh. The finely decorated Norman door, the plague plaque and war memorials cover the history of times past and present. The wooden poppy-headed benchends are renowned for their lively carvings and profusion of rabbits and dogs. Scholars came to see the 13th century carving over the north porch and enjoy the architectural styles within the church. Methodism was strong in the village an the tiny Primitive Methodist chapel still stands and is now used by the parish council. The present stone-built Methodist chapel, erected in 1908, replaced an earlier brick barn-like structure, now a branch of the County Library.

Today the children are fortunate to get their education until 18 years of age if required, in the village. The old Gibson charity school is now redundant and used for community purposes. An infant and junior school was built in the 1920s for an increasing population, and named after John Hunt, the missionary, who went to Fiji. The school retains a link with that far-away island which most youngsters will never see. By the 1960s another school was needed to serve a modern housing estate to the north of Main Street. This is called Chuter Ede, a name which amuses and puzzles the children. He was once a Minister of Education. Secondary education is catered for at The Grove comprehensive school with its adjacent leisure centre.

The New Hall on the southern outskirts, owned by the brewing families of Hardy and later Warwick, was purchased before the Second World War by the Ministry of Health to become a 'Mental Colony', as the OS map described it. Much good work and care for the mentally handicapped has been done here. Times change and the future of this wooded site is again under consideration.

Industries in the past were based on the land, vines, wool, ropemaking and gypsum. Only the latter survives, the gypsum being of very high quality and mined in large quantities on the perimeter of the village. The sound of blasting is a familiar one to a number of inhabitants. Pumps, light electrical work, the new 'starter workshops' and shops, now offer employment. There was a child clinic here in 1938, but only recently a doctor's surgery, dentist and chemist, long fought for by the village and parish council, have been opened.

The almshouses record a gift of Alice Bakewell in 1892 and house a number of elderly people in small but compact homes, now with 'mod cons'! A son of the parish was the actor Sir Donald Wolfit (1902–68), born to an old Nottinghamshire family; his father was a prosperous brewer's clerk living on the London Road. A plaque records his birthplace.

The wartime airfield from whence the gliders flew to Arnhem in the Second World War is now cultivated as farmland, a return to the peaceful occupation of the earlier inhabitants of Balderton.

Barnby In The Willows 🌿

The village was 'Barnbi' at the time of the Domesday Book. 'Willows' appears in 1575, possibly from the willows by the river Witham which runs through the village. However, no willows have grown here since 1900, and the old craft of basket making has disappeared.

The parish church of All Saints is situated at the very end of the village. There is a footpath through the churchyard which goes over a bridge, crossing the river and into Lincolnshire nearby. The church was built in 1267 and is unusual in that it has a nave and chancel of equal length.

Barnby does not have a through road, but the line of the old coach road from Newark to Sleaford can be found in the form of a track going east out of the village. This went out of use following the turnpiking and improving of the Newark to Leadenham road, which is the present A17.

Barnby is mainly a farming village wich much of the land and buildings belonging to Barnby Manor until more recent times, when cottages were sold to private individuals. At the moment there is a pig farm, a dairy cattle herd, several mixed farms, a stud and a racing stables.

The village has a craftsman in brass and two builders. Many villagers have large gardens and there is friendly rivalry amongst the vegetable growers at the yearly Horticultural Show.

Whilst in the past a large proportion of the population worked in the village, now the majority find employment in the surrounding towns. Since the 1960s a considerable number of new properties have been built in the village. Yet in spite of these new properties and the associated influx of people, Barnby has still managed to retain its village character.

The village had a beerhouse in 1864 in the name of Thomas Grocock. Now the village pub has the appropriate name of the Willow Tree. This is the meeting place of the darts, pool and skittles teams.

Barnby House still has part of the old village oven to be seen on the outside and as a feature on the inside.

The Jubilee Church of England school, dated 1850, is now the village hall. It was closed as a school in December 1963 and later bought by the Parish Council with the help of various grants.

In 1922 the village cricket team won the Hospital Cup with two families providing most of the players, namely the Vesseys and the Grococks. The bat used to open that match is still in the village.

The dovecote still stands in the village and is a listed building considered to be medieval.

Barnby Moor 🌿

In 1690 Ogilby's *Itinerary*, a book of road maps, showed the Great North Road or Old London Road running from West Drayton by Jockey House and on to Barnby Moor. Because of its isolation it was a paradise for highwaymen. As traffic increased, these sandy lanes were abandoned and the new road was made through Gamston, Retford and on to Barnby Moor in the mid 18th century. Now the A1 bypasses this route.

One find old coaching inn, the Blue Bell, always referred to as 'the Bell', is now widely known as the Olde Bell Hotel. This inn rose to fame when stage coaches started to run in the early 18th century. One traveller remarked that in 1714, there were so many coaches at the Bell that some were ill-put to find room. Its most notable landlord was Mr George Clark, a man of great personality, highly respected, a sportsman and a breeder of horses. Sylvanes, a well known sports writer, described him as 'the gentleman innkeeper'.

Travellers always looked forward to the first sight of the four elm trees which stood opposite the Bell. These were later cut down and the pond at their side filled in. There was stable room for 120 horses and beds for the postboys. If more stabling was needed the White Horse Inn also in the village was used. This still stands today. For a great number of years the Bell was a private residence, divided into two houses. At this time the village was without a church and part of the inn was used as a chapel.

Barnby Moor had a Mansion House and pleasure grounds in the 18th century. Mr Darcy Clark built Barnby Moor House on this site in the 1800s. Joshua Gladwin Jebb, grandfather of the current Lord Gladwin, purchased it in 1875. It was demolished in 1881 and a further one built in 1883. It is recorded that the vergers welcomed Gladwin Jebb's return but sadly he died in 1901. His son Sydney took over but, as he was given Firbeck Hall by his aunt and much preferred that, he sold the house to

Barnby Moor village

the Barber family who owned Harworth pit. During the second world war the Barbers' large entrance hall was used as a clinic for the young mothers to take their babies to be weighed and collect 'Virol'.

The 7th Earl Fitzwilliam purchased the Grove Hounds from the then Lord Galway in 1907. He was at that time also Master of the two family packs at Wentworth and Fitzwilliam together with the Coollattin in Ireland; probably a unique position. Since the amalgamation in 1952/3 with the Rufford Hounds, the Hunt is now called the Grove & Rufford Foxhounds. Originally the Kennels supported 70 couple of foxhounds with as many staff and horses as required. Urbanisation has meant some reduction in hunting and some has been sold or leased off, so now there is provision for four dwellings, kennels for 35 couple of foxhounds and seven stables. The Boxing Day Meet is now held at the Olde Bell Hotel.

The Earl Fitzwilliam also set land aside for the village hall to be built and a cricket pitch. The hall is still well looked after and used, but the cricket pitch has reverted back to grassland incorporated into the Kennels land.

The Pig Improvement Company now have a pig breeding farm which was formerly named 'College Chicks'. All the land once belonged to the Priory of Blyth which was taken by Henry VIII at the Dissolution of the Monasteries. It was later handed over as an endowment for his new foundation of Trinity College in the University of Cambridge.

The village has expanded but it is still one of the smallest in the county. Where men used to work on the farms, now most of them commute to different towns. The smithy has long since gone and the village shop, post office and church have all been altered to form private residences. The Reindeer Hotel is now an old people's home and they, like the Olde Bell and White Horse, have to draw staff from outside the village.

Barnstone 🦌

This is a small village in the south of the county. It is part of the parish of Langar-cum-Barnstone and lies between the Trent valley and the Belvoir hills. Originally a small farming community, it developed with the cement manufacturing company, which gave employment to many local inhabitants. Now, however, the scale of production has considerably reduced and as two new housing developments have been built, a new generation of commuters and employees in industry has developed on the old Langar airfield, enlarging the community.

It is quite active in its extra-mural facilities, with a Women's Institute who are active in improving rural life and environment. Scout groups and a very active and useful playgroup meets in the village hall.

The small village church, part of the larger parish church at Langar, hosts the fellowship group, a lively meeting of young and old from all the group churches. The pantomime, performed each year, is undertaken to raise money for the local churches.

Barton-in-Fabis 🦌

The village of Barton-in-Fabis belonged for many generations to the Lords Grey of Codnor. The last Lord Grey had no legitimate heirs, but in his will dated 1496, it stated he had several bastards, including two Harrys – the 'greate Harry' and 'little Harry'. To one of these Barton was left for a portion, and his daughter and heiress married one of the Derbyshire Sacheverells, who came and settled in Barton. He and his male descendants held the manor for 200 years. When the male line died out, the estate was carried by an heiress to the Cliftons.

There is a beautiful alabaster tomb in the chancel of the church which is of William Sacheverell (died 1616) and his wife Tabitha. The remains of the manor house is now a farmhouse, and is merely a fragment of the old mansion. The brick dovecote is still standing, and was repaired in 1986. The church of St George dates back to the 12th century, with an excellent high unaisled chancel of the late 14th century. A clerestory was added in the 15th century, and the porch was added in 1693. There has been extensive repair work to all parts of the church, including the complete overhaul and cleaning of the Sacheverells' tomb.

It is believed that in the 17th century Charles I crossed the Trent at Barton on the ferry, which is said to have been in existence since Roman times. This latter was substantiated when, in 1865, the discovery of a fragment of Roman pavement was found in Barton. Nowadays, the ferry only runs if you contact a gentleman across the river at Attenborough.

Besthorpe

By the village green and its oak tree stands the chapel of ease, Holy Trinity. The original chapel was converted into a school in 1734. When the present church was rebuilt in 1844, the village hall next door was built as a schoolroom. This in turn was replaced by the present school, opened in 1879. The twin chestnut trees in the playground were planted at about the same time, and the children of Besthorpe, Girton and South Scarle, the villages served by the school, have a long history of skill with conkers! The modernised village hall is used for village events, a youth club, and by the WI. The very large playing field is also used by these organisations and the school.

The old brickyard provided the mellow bricks of the older houses, though two are of stone. In Victorian times the manor housed 'a young gentlemen's boarding school'. Now, new development is expanding the village. The former windmill, unusually small, lies to the east.

The Lord Nelson Inn still provides good refreshment for travellers

The village school, Besthorpe

along the Newark to Gainsborough road, though the mounting block at the roadside is little used now.

Trent Lane leads to the river and gravel works. Here a wonderful variety of wild flowers grow undisturbed amongst the old workings. The former hamlet of Meering was situated at the end of this lane, and this was where the ferry took visitors across to Carlton-on-Trent. Now there is little contact with the other side of the river because the only way there is via the bridge at Newark, a journey of 20 miles.

A footpath at the north end of the village leads to the quiet open waters of the Fleet, where Herons from Besthorpe heronry join the fishermen.

Bestwood ✿

This village lies six miles to the north of the city centre of Nottingham and once formed part of the Royal hunting park of Bestwood. Plantagenet kings hunted here and built the first Bestwood Lodge. It was here that Richard III received the message that Henry Tudor had landed in Wales with an invasion army in August 1485. Richard left his beloved lodge and village and lost his crown and his life at the Battle of Bosworth Field.

Legend has it that Nell Gwynne and Charles II enjoyed visiting Bestwood and that Charles had a wager with Nell. He said she could have all the land she could ride around before breakfast. (Nell was not known for being an early riser.) However, she got up at the crack of dawn and, dropping handkerchiefs along the way, rode round the estate and returned in time for breakfast. Whether the story is true or not, Nell finished up owning the land and her son by Charles became the first Duke of St Albans. The names of the public houses in the area are reminders of Bestwood's history – Charles II, Nell Gwynne, Deerstalker, White Hart, Duke of St Albans, Royal Hunt and Harvesters.

In the 18th century the land was parcelled into farms and cultivated and only a small part of the land in Bestwood Park remained forested. The farmland to the south was eventually bought by the Nottinghamshire City Council and private developers. This part of the old Bestwood estate is now a vast residential area which includes Top Valley and Rise Park, and the present Bestwood Lodge is an hotel.

The Bestwood area had two of the cotton mills built on the river Leen by the Robinson family, namely Forge Mill (on the site of an old iron forge) and Middle Mill. The mills brought a working rather than a resident population. It was not until John Lancaster, under lease from the 10th Duke of St Albans in 1872, sank a coal mine, that a substantial number of people came to live in the village. The first colliery houses were built in 1876, there were 64 dwellings in all. The Bestwood Coal and Iron Company village was firmly established and the villagers all became dependent on the company. Over 2,000 men were employed by the company in its heyday, some travelling from nearby Bulwell, Arnold and Hucknall. There were enough men, just in Arnold, to form their own branch of the Nottinghamshire Miners Federation in 1881.

Until the 1920s the village housing was static but then there were continuing developments until 1950, when there was massive development. This increased the population for the local school from 67 pupils in 1948 to nearly 300 by 1960.

Due to the unrest of the labour force the ironworks was forced to close in 1928. The closing of the colliery in 1967 came as a terrific blow to the community and to the workforce from surrounding areas. The village continued its close connections with the coal industry, however, as the

South Notts Area HQ was based here, although they have now been moved and have been situated at Edwinstowe since 1985. British Coal area workshops still remain in Bestwood. The spoil heap has now been drained and grassed and is alive with flora. One could hardly visualise a pit ever being there.

Bestwood St Mark's mission church was built in 1887 at a cost of £1,746, the cost of which was donated by the Duke of St Albans and the Lancaster family. The first sermon was preached by Dr Ridding, the first Bishop of Southwell, who dedicated not only the church but also the newly opened village cemetery.

From the past industrial village, Bestwood has now become a very quiet village with an abundance of lovely country walks, especially through the Bestwood Country park.

Bilsthorpe 🎷

One of the earliest accounts of Bilsthorpe, Bilstrop or Bildstorp was in the 9th century when the Danes plundered the country. The old part of the village was around the church, and a cupboard still remains in the Hall, where Charles I was reputed to have hidden in the Civil War. This same Hall has been incorporated into a farm, opposite the church. Originally there were 43 houses and 217 inhabitants in the village.

Originally there were two moats, one of which can still be seen. Gravel pits were in existence for the purpose of repairing roads. The children attended a very tiny school and the post office was a wooden cottage (since modernised).

Employment in the village was largely farming, until 1922 when the Stanton Ironworks sank the pit. Men from different towns and villages were employed and were housed in wooden chalets. Tragedy came in the shape of an explosion, when men were severely injured and some lost their lives. The rector of the parish church and the manager of the colliery disagreed over compensation, consequently the manager built a wooden church in the 'new village' at a cost of £800. A rector was engaged, with the men and their familes being 'encouraged' to leave the parish church and attend the new one. The 'rectory' was opposite and is now the fish and chip shop.

The young man who played for the films in the village hall was ordered to also play the organ on Sundays, and the postmaster trained the choir. This situation remained until the pit was nationalised and the families drifted back to St Margaret's and the wooden building became the church hall, used for bazaars and Sunday school etc. At the present day the other main employers are a large farm involved in growing potatoes for crisp manufacturers, a factory which makes men's clothing, together with the headquarters of a major egg-producer, giving a fair number of villagers work.

The Stanton Arms public house was once the only building on the west of the main street and during the Second World War there were only fields between the colliery houses and the horizon. The bombing and flashes over Chesterfield could be seen quite clearly, with the searchlights crossing and re-crossing the sky. An occasional plane came down nearby and anyone who could run flocked to the scene, with parachute material being in great demand by would-be costumiers. Nissen huts sprang up overnight and air-raid shelters appeared like mushrooms in back gardens.

Rationing was ordered, so queueing became necessary. Soon the custom grew to gather at the little butcher's shop – it was only big enough for three customers at a time, with the others waiting outside. Often one person queueing would put down the baskets of her friends and neighbours. This didn't suit one irate customer and he kicked all the baskets into the gutter and defied anyone to replace them! Very often the moon was still high in the sky when the day's queueing began.

In about 1944 the church got a new electric organ – hitherto it had to be pumped by a little boy and if he got tired the tune sank lower and lower, until he had to be prodded awake.

Home Farm, a very important house in days gone by, has been modernised and made into a public house. A fine specimen tree stands on its threshold and has given it its name – The Copper Beech. Another innovation is the sauna and squash courts housed in the village hall, where aerobics and martial arts classes are also held.

In 1989, proposals to build a power station were announced, close to the pit to save transportation costs.

Bingham 🐾

The village of Bingham, which in reality is now more a small market town, has grown tremendously since the 1960s.

There are still memories of village characters from the past. One such lady is remembered for her kindness, till her death (in 1928) in her 99th year. Every day during the First World War, she would walk around

Bingham collecting potato peelings and vegetable waste, selling it to the pigkeepers. Every penny she received was given to the church. Her name was Ann Harrison and a wooden statue to her memory is to be found in the church.

Another inhabitant, known to all the village, was a man named Green who had a donkey. He never went anywhere without his donkey and was known as 'Donkey Green'. The cottage where he lived was known as Donkey Green Cottage and still is today, a little changed perhaps.

Present day inhabitants follow a multitude of jobs and professions, a good number commuting to Nottingham and some even as far away as London. There is an industrial estate which provides work for a lot of youngsters leaving school, as well as married women. In the centre of Bingham work is found in the shops, offices, hairdressing, library, health centre, school meals services and with tradesmen.

Cricket is still flourishing, first started at the turn of the century. There is a lovely story from the cricket field. A match was in progress when the fire siren started up. The man batting was a volunteer fireman. Down went his bat as he legged it for all his worth to the fire station and by the skin of his teeth just caught the tender. It was the longest run of the match!

In the 1970s the open market was started up again. Every Thursday sees a busy, bustling Bingham, crowds coming in from nearby villages and holidaymakers joining the locals. The Butter Cross looks down on the scene as it has done for many years.

Bleasby 🦢

Bleasby is a small, attractive village lying approximately one mile from the river Trent, which is approached down a narrow winding lane appropriately called 'Boat Lane'. The river offers such leisure pursuits as fishing, water-skiing and speed boat racing, with very pleasant walks along the tow paths. Refreshment on sunny, summer days can be obtained from the 18th-century Star and Garter hotel. Several holiday sites are to be found in this area.

There are a number of light industries in the village and the hamlets of Gibsmere and Goverton. There is a small market garden with caravan site, and a herb garden and crafts at Gibsmere, family builders, taxi services, farmhouse tea shop and a caravan site at the pub in Bleasby, and at Goverton, the dairy is to be found and, in her spare time, the 'milk lady' dresses dolls in satin and lace. The cottage industries of yesteryear – shoemaker, tailor, smithy, wheelwright, framework knitter, are long gone, although the cottages which housed these industries are still lived in. The majority of people commute to Nottingham, some twelve miles distant.

Farming is still carried on, mostly arable though with a sprinkling of cattle and sheep, but over the years a number of farms have been broken up and sold.

As a lasting memento of the Queen's Silver Jubilee, it was suggested that the worked out gravel pits be made into a conservation area. Hoveringham Group Ltd, who owned the land, welcomed the idea and eventually the area became known as the Jubilee Ponds. Undergrowth has been cleared, trees and shrubs planted, seats placed at strategic points and the whole area is now a small nature reserve for the enjoyment of residents.

Bleasby is a mixture of the old and new. The oldest (known as 'The Old House'!) is a 14th-century farmhouse, Manor Farm, noted for its dovecote. The pub, the Wagon & Horses, dates back to the 17th century.

The founder of the Salvation Army, William Booth, spent part of his early childhood at what is now known as 'Old Farm' and his sister Mary was baptised in the church.

In 1763 a whipping post was erected at Bleasby, at a cost of 2s 6d! Stocks were already in the village and had been used previously.

The day school was erected in 1855 and was in use until September 1961, when a new school was opened. The school has on register approximately 70 pupils from Bleasby, Thurgarton and Hoveringham. The original building is now used as a village hall.

An unofficial village meeting point is the well-stocked shop and post office, where one will often find villagers enjoying a chat whilst making their purchases.

The church, dedicated to St Mary the Virgin, offers a Sunday school and the choir, formed from members of the Trent group of parishes, sing at family and special services.

Blidworth 🎐

Blidworth, up on the hill, has a most marvellous view looking towards Nottingham. Gradually turning left in a circle, one can see in the distance Seely's Mansion, Belvoir Castle, Lincoln Cathedral, and still further left following the Trent, a whole line of power station cooling towers up towards Gainsborough.

Blidworth has looked over this view long before castle, cathedral and cooling towers were built. In fact it was a village before Domesday, self-contained and surrounded by forest. Much of the Robin Hood legend revolves round Blidworth. It was here, it is said, that the Maid Marion lived before her marriage to the outlaw. On the parish boundary at Fountaindale is Friar Tuck's Well, sadly in disrepair, with nearby the moated area on which the Friar had his home. Here it was that Robin had his famous fight on the bridge. There is little to be seen but one senses that this is where it really happened! Another of Robin Hood's loyal friends, Will Scarlett, is reputedly buried in Blidworth churchyard.

St Mary's church is also the scene for the unique annual Rocking ceremony, the origin of which goes back at least 400 years. Indeed it was at the revelries following the ceremony in 1598 that Thomas Leake met his death in a fight, all for the love of a 'lady'. Originally held to commemorate the Presentation of Christ in the Temple, the Rocking celebrations are now less boisterous affairs. The male child born in Blidworth parish nearest to Christmas Day is rocked in the beautiful flower-decked cradle at a special service in St Mary's on the first Sunday in February.

The village has always been involved in agriculture, but the Industrial Revolution brought the framework knitters, with at least 35 frames in use in Blidworth at one time. James Prior, in his book *Forest Folk*, a novel based on Blidworth, talked of the Luddite activities when frames in the village were smashed. This was based on fact. As Prior's hero, Tant Rideout, went to war, so did Blidworth's own hero, Matthew Clay, who fought at the battle of Waterloo. Full military honours were bestowed on him and many generals were present at his funeral in Bedford years later.

With the demise of framework knitting and the birth of the coal mining industry it was common for men to walk as far as Linby Colliery to work. Agriculture and its allied trades still predominated though, until well into this century. Education and religion went together, with both the Methodists and Church of England having their own school in the old village. For those who sought solace in liquid refreshment local hostelries abounded.

1925 saw the sinking of Blidworth pit and the start of a new era. The new village sprang up with families coming from all over the country, bringing with them a mingling of dialects and customs, new aspirations and new shops. The Church schools have closed and new council schools have been built to accommodate the increasing number of children. Agriculture has lost its dominance, with modern methods needing less manpower. However, mining is declining with the closure of the colliery in 1989 – will the Blidworth of the future become a commuter satellite?

Blyth

In 1988 the church and village of Blyth celebrated their ninth centenary. Many strangers and visitors came to join in the year-long programme of festivities, for hospitality to travellers has been the tradition and principal occupation of the village from the time of its founding.

The church was established by Sir Roger de Builli, the Norman overlord of Tickhill, and his wife Muriel. They chose Blyth, where the ground rises above a curve of the river Ryton, as the site for a Benedictine priory, a daughter house of the Abbey of Saint Katharine of Rouen. During the early Middle Ages the priory flourished. In later medieval times the village grew in importance as the priory declined and the Angel Inn took the place, for hospitality to travellers, of the priory gatehouse.

In the reign of King John, William Cressy of Hodsock built a hospital for lepers here after the disease had been brought from the Middle East by returning Crusaders and pilgrims. The building still stands. For many years it was the village school. In the Second World War it was used as a canteen and rest room for soldiers and more recently it has been converted into two dwellings.

The Tournament Field between Blyth and Styrrup, one of only five in England to be granted a royal licence, attracted thousands of visitors to the area, knights and noblemen, merchants and pedlars.

About the year 1400, when England was at war with France, King Henry IV severed the links between Blyth and Rouen. At this time the present church tower was built and the south aisle widened to form the nave of the parish church. But the Norman nave where the monks worshipped still remains, with its massive pillars and arches of Roche Abbey stone. To separate the parish church from the priory a barrier wall was erected at the end of this nave. It was painted with a great picture of the Last Judgement showing God seated on a rainbow throne with the dead rising from their coffins to be led to Heaven by the angels, or driven to Hell. At a later period the picture was whitewashed over, and for about 450 years remained hidden under a coat of limewash and grime.

During a thorough inspection of the church in 1985 this painting – the Doom – was rediscovered and the task was begun of revealing all the medieval figures, angels, saints, coffins, weapons and musical instruments. Now artists and historians from all over the world come to see the painting.

After the Dissolution of the Monasteries in Henry VIII's reign the Prior's lodging was converted into a gentleman's residence known as Blyth Abbey. Blyth expanded and prospered under the lordship of the Clifton family of Clifton and Hodsock. A great traveller and antiquarian of Tudor times, John Leland, declared that the name suited the nature of its inhabitants.

The first Blyth Hall was completed by Edward Mellish, a wine merchant, in 1689 on the site of the Abbey. One of the first visitors to the Hall was Celia Fiennes who admired the red brick mansion with its neat gardens.

The Mellish family remained at Blyth for two centuries, in every generation improving, modernising and expanding the Hall, church and village. The 18th century was a time of great prosperity, when the coaching inns served passengers travelling between Rotherham and Retford, London and the North. This was the period when people first spent holidays in Blyth.

In 1806 Colonel Henry Francis Mellish, a soldier of distinction and a friend of the Prince Regent, sold the Blyth estate – some say gambled it away – to Joshua Walker of Rotherham. The Walker family eventually sold the Hall to Francis Willey, a wool merchant of Bradford, who became Lord Barnby after the First World War. The Memorial Hall was built by Lord Barnby as a thank-offering for the safe return of his son from that war and in memory of those who died.

During Lord Barnby's time the Hall and grounds achieved a brief magnificence. The cricket field was created in the park, and Blyth Show became an important annual event which continued to attract exhibitors and visitors until Bank Holiday was moved to the end of August. This altered the pattern of the classes, and then a series of wet summers washed it out.

For a hundred years Blyth has been a popular venue for cyclists, being a pleasant ride out from Sheffield. Most of the visitors now come by car and keep four inns and a big restaurant in the parish quite busy. And now the Granada Service Station on the bypass keeps up the tradition of Blyth hospitality.

Bradmore 🌿

Bradmore is a small pleasant village on the A60 Loughborough road. It has long been connected with the neighbouring village of Bunny just down the road, since the Parkyns of Bunny purchased the village from the Willoughbys of Wollaton.

In July 1705 much of the village of Bradmore was burnt down, including the church, leaving the tower and steeple still standing. The church was never rebuilt and eventually the vicar of Bunny became the vicar of Bradmore also. Some of the farmhouses in Bradmore today show the evidence of Sir Thomas Parkyns' architecture and one of the farmhouses has the initials 'Sir T.P. 1736' in the brickwork.

Around 1830 most rural businesses were represented in this truly rural village – there was a public house, malt rooms, two shops, blacksmiths, a joiner and undertaker, wheelwright, shoemaker, saddler and baker. A thriving and busy village with two windmills, one was actually moved, it is said without the sails, to the side of the main road to Ruddington. The last miller was named Treece and the field where the mill stood is called 'Treece's Close'. Several other fields around Bradmore have unusual names, such as 'Labour in Vain', 'Peet's Wife's Nook', 'Isaac's Nine acre', 'Dead Man's Grove', 'Froghole', 'Long Wells', 'Crock Hill' etc. Sadly at the present time the village is far les self-sufficient and self-supporting than in the past. Only a couple of working farms still remain and most of the villagers are either retired, or commute to neighbouring towns.

Brinsley 🌿

Brinsley is a very pretty village, especially on the west side with its panoramic views. To the south side however the lovely walks and paths have been obliterated by overflowing slush sent over from a colliery coal washery. The looming piles of silt cover hundreds of acres of land and property, thus changing the horizon view.

In the 12th century two outstanding residences were built for the Duke of Devonshire. The Hall and the Manor both now exist as farms, but they still carry many of their original features.

Early in the 19th century crofters came and settled in the district. Land was claimed by energetic men, who built their houses not facing the road. Several of these houses can be seen in Cordy and Church Lanes.

The occasional finding of Brinsley bricks indicates that at some time there must have been a brickyard here. Pollington colliery closed in 1919, and the other colliery called Bodtod closed later. The site is now a picnic area. Before the Bodtod headstocks were removed the area was used for the filming of D. H. Lawrence's *Sons and Lovers*. Many Brinsley residents were used as 'extras'.

Brinsley has a pretty church. Built in 1847 and controlled by Greasley, it was called St Saviour's, but later changed to St James'. In 1881 a resident vicar Mr Percival Page was appointed, his weekly wage £4. It once also boasted three chapels, two Wesleyan, the other Methodist, but now only one resited chapel remains. In those early days, on anniversary Sundays, competition was rife as to which chapel would realise the most money. Brinsley Church school was built in 1849, and a smaller one, St John's, built a little later.

The village had as many as ten public houses at one time but now only five remain. The eldest one is a coach house called the Robin Hood. In 1940 during the removing of a fireplace some very ancient bills were discovered. Whisky cost 6s 2d for five gallons, and sheep cost only 7s 6d each!

Like most villages, Brinsley has had its minor scandals, but a special meaty one comes to mind. During the Second World War, a neighbouring villager had a 20 stone pig killed, leaving it overnight in his outhouse. By morning the pig had disappeared, leaving no trace. Suspicion fell on the Brinsley area. Innuendos were rife, but the mystery remains to this day. Not a pig's trotter was found, or even a pork chop!

About 1970 the population of Brinsley increased sharply and is now about 5,000, which calls for a mention of the Brinsley tote fund. For many years this hard-working committee have given trips, and one year, a Christmas gift to nearly 600 pensioners.

Bulcote 🌿

Along the A612 Southwell to Nottingham road between Burton Joyce and Lowdham is a sign which says 'Bulcote Village' and that, as far as most people are concerned, is all they know of Bulcote. They may not know for instance, that the village was mentioned in the Domesday Book, where it is recorded that the population included 'eight freemen,

Ivy House, formerly the Unicorn, Bulcote

eleven villagers, twelve smallholders and two slaves with three ploughs'. The only ancient building of any size is now the church. The original foundation of this dates from the 13th century and it was built by the Santa Maria family, who owned the manor. This church collapsed in 1862 and a new one was built on the same foundations. Dedicated to the Holy Trinity, the church retains the 1662 liturgy and attracts worshippers beyond the confines of the village.

The 17th and 18th centuries saw great change in the village, many substantial houses being built along the old main road, including the manor house which though dating from 1708, was erected on an earlier foundation.

The former public house, the Unicorn, closed and as a private residence was named 'Ivy House'. This building was reputed to be haunted. There were also a general shop, pork butcher's and a young ladies school at Bulcote Lodge. All have now disappeared, though the Unicorn re-opens its doors occasionally and, with a one-day licence, becomes once more a village pub. This colourful event is in aid of the church and is a popular occasion.

It is fair to say that 'modern' Bulcote dates from the Queen's coronation year of 1953 when the village, as a community, really 'took off'. In that year a social committee was formed to organize events and many residents well remember helping to fashion 4,000 pink paper roses to adorn the hedges and recall the production of *A Midsummer Night's Dream* performed on the manor house lawns. There are many activities now promoted by this hard working committee. There is a also a thriving cricket club which has attracted so many members that they were able to stage a match between old and new Bulcote.

Bunny 🦢

The name has nothing to do with rabbits, but comes from an old English term for the reeds or long grasses that grew around the area.

Bunny nurtured one of the most endearing eccentrics of the 18th century, a classical scholar, mathematician, lawyer, amateur architect, squire and benefactor of the villages of Bunny and Bradmore, a neighbouring village. Thomas Parkyns, a member of the Parkyns family connected with the village from 1570, did a great many things for Bunny. He designed and built many of the farmhouses in the district, some of which are still standing today. One of his most famous projects was the wall built around Bunny Hall, which he built on a series of arches.

He erected the old school house and almshouses at a cost of £400, and people passing through the village today stop and read the inscription over the south doorway, carved in stone and topped by an unusual pineapple shape. There is also an inscription over the north doorway. Lady Anne Parkyns, Sir Thomas's mother, wished to make provision for the instruction of poor children in the knowledge of God and also teach them the three Rs. Sir Thomas also left money for widows and funds for apprenticing boys for trades, and these charities are still in existence today.

Sir Thomas found time in his busy life for sport and is affectionately called the 'Wrestling Baronet'. An annual wrestling match was established by him in 1712 on Midsummer's Day, and many came from far and near to witness these matches. They went on for 99 years, long after his death. A gold laced hat was the first prize valued at 22s, and 3s was the second. He often competed himself, and so did his footman and coachman. So keen was he on wrestling that he designed his own monument, which today stands in the fine parish church often referred to as 'The Cathedral of the Wolds'. His monument depicts him in a life size wrestling stance, and is well worth a visit.

His grandson was created Lord Rancliffe (in the peerage of Ireland) but the 2nd Lord Rancliffe died childless in 1850, leaving the property to his mistress. It has since passed through many hands. Sadly the likes of Sir Thomas will probably never be seen again.

Burton Joyce ✌

Burton Joyce is a village on the banks of the river Trent, situated about five miles from Nottingham. At the time of the Norman conquest it was a small village with various ways of spelling Burton (Byrton, Birten) and later Jorz was added as the then chief landowners were the de Jorz family.

As more building land became available the village grew in size, the main landowner now being the 5th Earl of Carnarvon (later to become famous as the discoverer of the Tomb of Tutankhamen). The Carnarvon Reading Room, now used by the Youth Club, retains his name, as does Carnarvon Drive.

Being on the main Nottingham to Lincoln railway line is an asset, but the village is well served with buses, while most commuters have their own transport. With the construction of the bypass (now Church Road) in 1931), the old village was cut off from the river but many interesting walks can be taken down there and in season the banks are a fisherman's paradise!

Many old buildings can be found around the village, including the manor house and the old stockingers' cottages – many still featuring the original long windows. The four churches all unite for various services, each having their own church hall which can be used for numerous activities.

Since the 1960s, Burton Joyce has grown considerably and it was necessary in 1962 to build the new school in Padleys Lane as the village hall had been used as an infants department during and since the Second World War, and this along with the village school was not adequate for the now growing population. However, the old village school is now used by the British Trust for Conservation Volunteers and the primary school children are in the Padleys Lane site.

The village is well equipped with shops, a bank, building society, post office and library.

There is a long connection with village crafts. Many men worked on the land whilst others used to be framework knitters and some of their wives were stocking seamers who sewed for Royalty. Many a story is told of how the finished stockings were taken over to Lambley to a collecting point, thence to Nottingham by carriers' cart, with the children accompanying their mothers over the Bridle Path before going to school.

Calverton 🦚

The population of Calverton, approximately 1,000 at the turn of the century, had risen to almost seven times that at the 1981 census. The Domesday Book states that in 1086 the village had a church and a priest, but no part of the present church is dated before 1120, although it almost certainly occupies the same site as the Saxon building and is dedicated to St Wilfrid.

Calverton's most famous son is undoubtedly William Lee, the inventor in 1589 of the stocking frame. His influence can still be seen in some of the old stockingers' cottages – with windows specially designed to give maximum light to the stocking frame. General Sir John Sherbrooke, hero of the Peninsular War and later Governor-General of Canada, lived in the village and although his body lies in the family vault at Oxton, there is a memorial to him in St Wilfrid's church.

An eccentric Calvertonian was John Roe, founder of a religious sect in the late 18th century. Amongst their customs was the method of choosing marriage partners by casting lots. Baptisms were held in the pool (now dried up) in Johnny Roe's garden. He was also responsible for developing a fine plum which goes by his name and which is still grown locally.

There are two ancient charities. A charity for the poor was started by Jane Pepper (who also gave a silver alms dish to the church) which was augmented by a bequest and a gift of land in the 18th century at the time of the Enclosures Act. (This was to compensate the poor for the loss of rights on Burner Common.) The Jonathon Labray Trust was set up by his will of 1718 and provides almshouses and, until 1973, a school. The school building is now used by the Scouts and Guides.

A church Sunday school was built on Burner Pool in 1846 and became the first day school. It was converted in 1852 and became the National school. In 1892 a public elementary school was erected. This is now St Wilfrid's Church of England primary school.

The village has a thriving cricket club with a long history. Cricket is believed to have been played as early as 1840 but there is no documentary proof until 1869. Several players have had distinguished careers at county level. In 1879 cricket was played on the ice at Salterford Dam, such was the enthusiasm of the players.

Calverton Colliery, started in 1937 but put 'on ice' during the Second World War, was the first mine to be officially opened under nationalisation in 1952. The first ever Miners' Welfare, Ladies' section was formed in Calverton. The new mine brought publicity and a new population. The new council estate and the Coal Board housing estate resulted in a new shopping centre and other facilities which in turn have attracted private building and industry. Many clubs and societies thrive in this energetic community.

Car Colston 🌿

Car Colston is a real country village in a conservation area, unspoilt by modern development. Steeped in history, it is situated one mile east of the A46, the old Roman Fosse Way, about twelve miles from Nottingham and eight miles from Newark.

The population today is 165, only a quarter of what it was a hundred years ago, housed in largely separate buildings set in their own grounds or informal groups of small cottages, mainly around a large open green and the village road near the church.

The village's special character lies in its two village greens, with views across the surrounding countryside towards Kneeton Hills over the Fosse Way, also over the vale to Belvoir Castle, eight miles away.

The Large Green is 16½ acres (the largest in the county) and Little Green at the other end of the village is 5½ acres. These greens originated in the reign of Queen Elizabeth I. Individual strips were cultivated by individual villagers, still recognised by their ridge and furrow appearance. In 1598 the freeholders agreed to the parish being enclosed, into fields as we know today, leaving the greens open so that cottagers could graze their horses, cows and geese. These rights are still in use and the

Common Rights Committee deals severely with any cottager who flouts the laws. Three exits from the village show posts, now minus their gates.

Car Colston was the home of Dr Robert Thoroton who published his *Antiquities of Nottinghamshire* in 1677, the first major history of Nottinghamshire. Since 1863 his stone coffin, dated 21st November 1678, has been in the church of St Mary at the west end of the north aisle, having been discovered below the surface in 1845 and opened while the chancel was under repair.

After the First World War the ecclesiastical parishes of Car Colston and Screveton were joined together. They share the village hall, Women's Institute, Football Club and Cricket Club. The village school closed in 1965 and children from both villages are bussed five miles away to the market town of Bingham. Mrs Emma Martin was the village post-mistress. Now Mary, her 80 year old granddaughter allows the same room to be opened on to the street for use as a post office two hours a week.

The Royal Oak public house on the village green is host to the South Notts Hunt every Boxing Day, when up to 150 horses and 3,000 spectators turn out to support the Meet.

The Feast of St Mary is held the weekend after 15th June. Until the First World War a village fair was held in celebration. In 1967 and 1972 this festival was revived. Now the church organises an event such as Gardens Open Day or supper in the village hall, always followed by a special church service. The church, 14th century, is renowned for its beautiful floral decorations on every festivity. The south chancel window, restored in 1988, is a fine example of Kempe's early work in stained glass. Each Rogation Sunday Car Colston and Screveton villages take turns to go in procession to a cornfield, where a Blessing of the Crops service is conducted.

The remains of a Roman villa are in a field next to the public house. Ground indentations are visible, but the foundations can only be seen from an aerial view. Situated in the corner of the green outside the walled gardens of Beech Close, a Queen Anne 18th century building, are the village stocks, still usable. Brunsell Hall, a 17th century brick manor house and Hall Farm both stand in walled gardens.

Forty years ago cricket didn't commence until cow pats were removed from the pitch. Cows stopped play whilst Joe Gilbert drove his herd from The Moors, home for milking. Once milked he returned to play his innings. Sons and grandsons from the Gilbert, Willis, Marsh and Barker families continue the cricket tradition, played since the 18th century.

37

On a still day church bells can be heard from Screveton, Bingham and Whatton. A rhyme passed on 50 years ago by Mr Jack Bates is:

> Colston's cracked pancheons
> Screveton's egg shells
> Bingham's toll rollers
> Whatton's merry bells.

Carlton-in-Lindrick 🌿

Carlton-in-Lindrick consists of two villages, South Carlton (Carlton Barron) and North Carlton (originally Kingston-in-Carlton).

The Domesday Book suggests that South Carlton was a Saxon village with a mill and a church. Possibly, there was an even older settlement. The church, with Saxon stonework and Saxon windows in the tower, also houses the Becket Altar with four carved crosses and a lead sealed relic.

Outside the church door stands the 'Devil Stone'. This is probably an old font and according to local legend, has been responsible for ill-fortune falling on people who tried to put it to secular use.

The sinking of the nearby Firbeck Colliery in the 1920s changed life in the village. Some young farm labourers had already decided to seek employment in the neighbouring pit and this was an added incentive to change occupations.

New housing development now began in Carlton, although the first houses were without mains water and electricity. As development progressed during the 1930s, the amenities soon arrived, although for many years old cottages still had rather primitive sanitation.

Until the Second World War life in the village continued under the benevolent eye of the Ramsden family.

The annual school treat at the Ramsden home, Wigthorpe Hall, is still talked about by the pre-war generation. Each springtime the children were invited on 'Daffodil' Saturday, to pick the flowers. No restrictions were placed on the numbers taken as the children staggered home with great armfuls.

The Methodists enjoyed their annual treat at Whitsuntide. The Sunday school Anniversary held on Whit Sunday, when the children sang their hymns and recited their poems, was followed the next day by a parade round the village. The children, dressed in their best, rode round on

The Mill House, Carlton-in-Lindrick

drays. Tea followed, after which games were played in the nearby field until late evening. Church choir and Sunday school members would sometimes transfer their allegiance for a few weeks prior to, and after the event. This could also happen when Sunday school outings were organised!

The village school, now officially known as the Ramsden School, was started in the 1830s, financed by the Ramsdens, augmented later by a state grant. Parents too, paid a small weekly amount. It was undenominational until 1894 when the Church took control.

Although officially Anglican, with the exception of one squire who joined the Plymouth Brethren, the Ramsden family worked well with the Methodists. A small cemetery is in the little copse at the back of the school. Their meeting house still stands.

Two charities, peculiar to Carlton, have now become one. The older one developed as a result of the Enclosure Act. This allocated land on the green for cottages and allotments at a nominal rent. The other, funded by

39

the Johnsons, provided an income to clothe and maintain 40 poor people. Today the old cottages have been replaced, while each pensioner in Carlton receives an annual voucher for £2 to be exchanged for goods in any Carlton shop.

Carlton had its share of eccentrics, perhaps the most notable being the Stanleys, who sold newspapers. They also had a small sweet shop, the 'shop' being a table, on which also reposed at least two cats, and a hat in which the hens laid their eggs. Upstairs was the 'maternity ward' for their various animals!

A small isolation hospital, now used by the Bassetlaw District Council, stands on the outskirts of the village. Lighting was then provided by lamps, while a centrally placed stove, fuelled by the ward maids during the day and the nurses at night, provided heat.

Apart from the usual village craftsmen, Carlton had a high class joinery and carpentry business, started by the Drabble brothers. Mr Fred Hanstock built up a cycle making and repairing business which eventually became Carlton Cycles, until taken over by Raleigh.

The Carlton Daffodil was developed by local gardeners and Carlton was also known as the 'Rose Village'.

The mill after being worked until after the Second World War, is now restored and houses a small museum of local artefacts.

Carlton has grown since 1945. The closure of Firbeck Colliery has changed the employment pattern. An industrial estate has been developed. Although there is still farming and colliery work, many of the newer residents commute.

Carlton-on-Trent 🦌

The village of Carlton stands on the west bank of the river Trent. The wharf, which is now little used, served the gravel and the malt trades which flourished in the 19th and first half of the 20th centuries. The village is situated on the old Great North Road, seven miles north of Newark. The Bell Inn, an old coaching inn, stands in the centre of the village but is now private residences. The original cobbles of the courtyard by the south entrance can still be seen.

The two most memorable features of the village are the lofty and very graceful spire of the church and also the old forge, now a private residence. It bears a brick horseshoe surrounding a doggerel rhyme which reads thus:

Gentlemen as you pass by,
On this shoe pray cast an eye,
If it be too straight, I'll make it wider,
If lame from shoeing, as they often are,
I'll have them eased with the greatest care.'

This sign is identical with one at Gonalston.

The parish church of St Mary the Virgin was built on the site of a chapel of ease of great antiquity, which served as a halting place for prayer and refreshment by the monks in pre-Reformation times as they journeyed on foot to the mother church at Lincoln. They forded the Trent at Carlton. The ancient building was razed to the ground in 1849 and the present church was dedicated in 1852.

Carlton Hall, formerly known as Carlton House, was built in 1765, in the Georgian style and is the home of the Vere-Laurie family. The south wing contains the beautiful Adam drawing room. It may be viewed, strictly by appointment.

Caunton

Caunton was mentioned in the Domesday book of 1086, with its original spelling of Calneton, which is still in use locally. It lies beside a willow-bordered beck, just off the Newark to Ollerton road, with its red brick houses and small grey church.

It is the village of the man who Tennyson called 'The Rose King'. Samuel Reynolds Hole lived at Caunton Manor as vicar and squire before serving as Dean of Rochester. Here he studied his beloved roses, and made himself the most famous of all amateur rose growers. In 1851 he recorded that he had 1,027 trees with over 400 varieties.

In his 19th century *Memories* Dean Hole writes of the custom, still recalled by older inhabitants, of 'The Rang-Tang'. If a villager persistently ill-treated his wife and family, a band of performers on penny trumpets, horns, old kettles, pokers and fire shovels would meet under his window at night to serenade him with derisive verses such as:

'There is a man in our town
Hodge Podge is his name.
He's been beating his good wife
Don't you think it a shame?

It's not because she's icy
It's not because she's lame.
She wants to wear the breeches
That's her little game.'

After three nights of serenading, they would burn an effigy of the offender, and often toll the church bell.

From *The Miracles of King Henry VI* comes one of the first references to the game of football. William Bartram of Caunton was kicked and injured during a game, but suddenly recovered when he saw the glorious King Henry VI in a vision. The game was called the foot-ball-game, 'one in which young men propel a huge ball, not by throwing it in the air, but by striking it and rolling it along the ground with their feet.'

St Andrew's church was rebuilt by the Normans in 1200 and so it remains today. In 1830 the church was in an appalling state of dilapida-

The Twitchell, Caunton

42

tion, with the altar, a box, only used as a resting place for the visiting curate's hat, crop and gloves. In 1869 Dean Hole put in hand a thorough restoration, and in 1989, a decorative panel and Victorian inscription over the chancel arch was uncovered. The ship's crest and lifebelt in the church are those of HMS *Caunton*, a coastal minesweeper, now decommissioned, but until 1955 the venue of several village visits.

During the earlier part of the 20th century, Caunton's life was dominated by the life and work of the farming community. Here children helped with the stooking of the sheaves at harvest time, chasing the rabbits for mothers to make into pies, and watched the annual visit of the threshing machine, with this time the mice being the target of their chase. They visited the mill, where the Sharp brothers baked the village bread, and the workshop of Ted Gilbert, the local joiner and wheelwright where they viewed with morbid curiosity the coffins made there. The church children envied the Methodist Chapel Anniversary when the children dressed in new clothes, paraded the village on a decorated dray, singing their choruses – or was it the tea party and the singing games they played afterwards, which were envied more? The church Sunday School had an annual trip to the seaside, and what excitement that was – a bus trip to 'Skeggie' (Skegness).

The two local pubs were other centres of community life. Here George entertained all comers with his rendering of *Underneath the Spreading Chestnut Tree*, in the hope of a free pint. Darts, dominoes and skittles were keenly contested, and Jock sat in his favourite corner playing Scottish airs on his mouth organ before walking home across the fields.

Children fished for Bullyheads and tiddlers in the beck and learned to swim at Bathleyford Bridge. They roamed the fields and woods collecting primroses, violets and bluebells in their season, and the church at Eastertime was filled with their posies.

Today Caunton seemingly appears the same, a few extra houses have been built, but the children now attend a modern school with all amenities, not the old building with its black stove, where the lucky ones baked, while those at the back froze. Today there is a playing field with cricket pitch and two tennis courts. The school hall is the venue for many village activities.

Clarborough

The long straggling village of Clarborough and the tiny hamlet of Welham are situated on the A620 between Retford and Gainsborough on the way to the east coast. Welham is an ancient spa. The spring which bubbles up beneath Well House in Bone Mill Lane was by 1700 called St John's Well and was renowned as a healing spa.

A railway line also runs through Clarborough and Welham taking passengers to Lincoln and the coast, and coal to West Burton power station. The railway passes through a tunnel in the area of Whinley's Farm, the tunnel top providing a most attractive asset to the village in the form of a nature reserve.

Clarborough Hill has many public footpaths crossing it and from certain vantage points, views across the plains to Lincolnshire in the east and towards Sheffield and Derbyshire in the west are well worth the walk. On clear days it is possible to see Lincoln Cathedral. On the northern boundary of the village is the Chesterfield Canal. This provides a towpath walk and some good angling. The canal is busy in the summer months with the passage of boats, some stopping at the Gate Inn for refreshments.

During 1966 Clarborough was declared a 'growth area' by the County Council and it has increased its size by about two-thirds, with a present population of around 1,600. New housing estates have been built in the Smeath Lane and Big Lane areas, development which meant the village schools were inadequate, causing the existing school to be extended. The institute on Church Lane also became too small for the ever-growing population and with money raised by the Community Association a new village hall was built. The land was acquired for the village by the Parish Council and the Playing Fields Committee has been very active in raising funds to provide the swings and slides there. There are many thriving organisations which cater for the needs of all ages.

At one point in its history the village thought it might become a miniature Dallas when British Petroleum did some test drilling for oil. The rig which was erected on top of Clarborough Hill was very spectacular when lit at night.

Mention must be made of the church's verger and sexton who has served for 35 years at St John the Baptist. Worshippers are summoned to church by the three bells rung solely by the verger – one in each hand and one on his foot. When he retired from grave-digging, a few years ago, he had dug 5,800 graves in parishes throughout Nottinghamshire.

The village is served by a post office combined with a newsagent's and general shop. There is also, just off Church Lane, a small industrial estate which has developed without intruding on the environment. The main industry in the past was agriculture and horticulture, but now there are only half a dozen farmers and four smallholders. These employ very few people and the main employers nowadays are the Central Electricity Generating Board at West Burton, Cottam Power Station and Rampton Hospital. In fact Clarborough has become a dormitory village, which has affected village life.

Collingham 🌿

Collingham was originally a Saxon settlement, which developed into the twin villages of North and South Collingham. In 1974 they united under one Parish council to become the present village with about 3,000 inhabitants.

Farming was a principal employer of labour and there was also a wide selection of trades. A directory of 1884 lists saddlers, cobblers, corn millers, maltsters, wheelwrights, tailors, surgeons, blacksmiths, carriers and many shopkeepers. As the population has grown these trades and services have decreased until there are now only the shopkeepers, and a health centre has taken the place of the surgeons. All that is left of the chemist's shop is an old sign advertising Hikit Health Salts, an invention of Mr Jones a previous chemist.

The osier beds which supplied local basket makers with willow have disappeared as the river Trent has been dredged and a new flood bank built. The flood marks on the north churchyard wall show how Colling-ham used to be flooded, and the church and graveyard were built on a mound. Children no longer gather and bunch cowslips to send off by the 8.15 mail train to London to be distributed round hospitals by the Bible Flower Mission. However, there is a regular bus service and the railway line is as important as ever. Local carrots were washed at the station before being sent to market in straw-lined wagons, and rabbits and poultry were kept overnight in the waiting room ready for Collingham Show day. This is one of the oldest shows in the county, having been started in 1841 by Collingham Farmers Club as a ploughing match and gradually developing into its present format.

Schools were to be found in both villages during the 19th century, largely run by the churches of many denominations. There were also private and boarding schools, one run by the daughters of the rector of South Collingham. Eventually the state took over the running of primary education and in 1962 a new school, the John Blow primary school was built and all pupils transferred there. Woodhill secondary school was opened in 1954 and closed in 1977.

Social life in the village was always well catered for with many clubs and societies. Among the oldest is the cricket club, still playing on the Dale Field given to the village by the Curtis family, noted benefactors in many ways. There is also a bowling club, tennis club, football club and badminton club, but the hockey club no longer functions. The pig club was once a flourishing organisation. All the pigs were killed by Jack Body, the local pig killer.

Seven public houses, now reduced to three, ran sick and dividing clubs. Members paid in each week, receiving a small sum when ill, and the residue was divided at Christmas. The Jolly Barge pub on the river Trent was used by bargees, some of whom would be bringing coal to Collingham wharf, and the Railway Inn by navvies building the railway line.

Two of the outstanding monuments in the village were the Saxon cross, which can still be seen at the north end of the village, and the elm tree planted on Stocks Hill in 1746. Unfortunately this succumbed to Dutch Elm disease in 1987 and has been replaced by an English oak.

Colston Bassett ❧

Colston Bassett is a small picturesque village on the Nottinghamshire/ Leicestershire border lands gently washed by the river Smite. To the west, some distance removed lies the ancient Roman Fosse Way while to the southeast the magnificent panorama of the Vale of Belvoir unfolds, with views extending over lush pasture to wooded hills, Belvoir Castle and into Lincolnshire beyond.

Over the centuries land has been husbanded by a number of great families. From the time of Henry I until the death of the last Lord Ralph Bassett the family of that name were Lords of this Manor, the village being known as Colston Bassett to distinguish it from Drayton Bassett in Staffordshire.

It has known its share of visitations by the grim reaper in plague, pestilence and in the Civil War, insurrection; many skirmishes having been fought within the village boundaries and neighbouring parishes. Indeed Manor Farm, built by the Hacker family in 1625, can claim to have had two brothers under its steep roofs, one loyal to the King, and the other, Francis, a Roundhead, addressed with the duty of arresting Charles I and then guarding and escorting him to a honed edge and a hungry scaffold in 1649.

Colston Bassett Hall is passed on the left as the road falls gently through a wooded cutting to the Smite bridge and on into the village. The centre is dominated by the village Cross, dating back to medieval times; mainly restored in 1831, it is one of only two properties kept by the National Trust in Nottinghamshire.

A short walk past the Inn up School Lane, reveals our village school where generations of children have danced around the Walnut tree at summer fetes.

The church, St John the Divine, rises loftily above surrounding trees. Designed by A. W. Brewill it is built in Victorian Gothic style.

Farming is still a predominant occupation although over the years change has seen smallholdings merging to produce larger highly mechanised estates and tenancies. This modernisation has led to a decline in the numbers of people employed on the land and a consequent loss of traditional village skills. Nevertheless, as the population has fluctuated, new residents have moved in, some commuting to their work in nearby towns but glad to return home to their village at the end of a busy day.

Colston Bassett has taken change in its stride and enjoys a thriving community life centred on the church and school. Unspoilt, drawing in the best of the new while retaining the best of the past.

Costock 🌿

Costock, lying on the borders of Nottinghamshire and Leicestershire, is still an unspoiled village.

One of its old buildings was the old windmill situated on East Leake Road. Unfortunately, it became dangerous and was finally demolished in about 1937. When in use it played a very important part in the life of the village. Corn was grown in fields in villages around the mill and taken to a barn in the village to be threshed. In those days this was done by flailing. It then went back to the mill to be ground into flour. This was then used at the farms around and at the village bakehouse. The mill is now replaced by a shed which appears to have some of the original small sized bricks in its structure.

The miller's barn, dating back to 1763, has now been converted into a house, but many of its old structural features still remain. At a later date when the windmill became unavailable, the grinding was also done in the barn and the old stone for the engine was still there when the conversion was done.

Costock was at one time the centre of a stocking framework knitting industry, and there were frames in all three shops. One was at the old bakery, which has now been converted into a house and was originally built as a malthouse. Another shop was at the bottom of the field opening out onto Millers Lane. The finished products were taken to Nottingham by horse and dray. Other Costock residents went to work at the basket works in East Leake, although there were also two blacksmith's shops and a small brickyard in the village.

The church, dedicated to St Giles, was built around 1200 of stone from the quarry in the neighbouring village of Wysall. There is a tomb, probably belonging to a knight, on the outside of the south wall, worn away over the centuries and at some time used for the sharpening of knives and swords. The marks are very clear today.

Costock has a lovely manor house. The land and money for its building was given to the chef of Elizabeth I on his retirement. The oldest house is Hall Farm House, the stone for which came from the same source as the church. It has stone mullioned windows and walls three feet thick. An open fireplace inside this house is ten feet long and has stones cut in a Tudor arch style very similar to the fireplace in the kitchen of Hampton Court. Many alterations were made in the 18th century. It is no longer a working farm. The last farmer who lived there had no children and the house and land were sold separately. During the occupation of the present owner the house has been refaced with Northamptonshire stone and reroofed.

Cotgrave 🍂

In June 1984, archaeologists started to excavate an Anglo-Saxon burial ground on Mill Hill, the highest point in Cotgrave. Skeletons of some 74 adults and 13 children dating from the second half of the 6th century AD were uncovered. With one of the male skeletons were the remains of a shield and spear.

Adjacent to this ancient burial ground stood Cotgrave's old post mill, site of another of Cotgrave's unsolved historical mysteries. One of its millers mysteriously disappeared after being accused of pilfering the villagers' corn. In the early part of the 19th century, it was rumoured that a body had been discovered in the vicinity of the mill foundations. Despite thinking that the body might be that of the missing miller, the villagers kept quiet and, strangely, never investigated the rumour. In 1972, pupils of Rushcliffe comprehensive school's archaeology group excavated the site of the old post mill. Parts of an adult male skeleton were found, showing that the cause of death may have been a sharp blow to the back of the head! Was the 'missing' miller murdered and had his body been found at last?

> 'Our sweet little village has qualities rare
> No village with it in the Shire can compare'

So wrote 'Rusticus' (George Hickling, 1827–1909), the village's well-known and much loved poet who was a framework knitter by trade. Volumes of his work can be found in the Local Studies Collection of Nottinghamshire County Library. The majority of his poems are descriptive and reflective pieces suggested by everyday events and scenes around the village of Cotgrave, where he lived all his life.

Geologically, Cotgrave used to be famous for Keuper Marl, the fine-grained sedimentary rock consisting of clay minerals, calcium carbonate and silt, which was exported for use on wickets of cricket grounds the world over.

The parish church of All Saints, dedicated on All Hallows Day in 1246, has always played an important role in village life. A week-long Festival of Village Life, centred around the church, is held every three years.

A great change came over the village in 1963 when Cotgrave's colliery, the National Coal Board's showplace for a number of years, came into production. Prior to this, Cotgrave's population had been approximately 600 and, within the short space of 18 months, the population rose to 6,000 when miners from all over the country, especially the North-East, came to live in the village with the promise of employment for the next 100 years. Work was provided for 1,500 men and a large housing estate was built to accommodate their families, together with shops, schools, a health centre and sports and social facilities. The bright future of Cotgrave Colliery, however, was sadly misjudged owing to major geological faults and in 1989 the original workforce of 1,500 was cut to 500. The effects this will have on village life as a whole remain to be seen.

Cropwell Bishop 🌿

Cropwell Bishop is a snug little village on the edge of the Vale of Belvoir.

The village has had a population explosion during the last 50 years. Any doubts of the old residents at the beginning of the developments have gone, because Cropwell Bishop has profited with shops and amenities and today is a well developed and stimulating district.

The oldest building is the beautiful church dedicated to St Giles, dating back to 1215.

Walking through the village, it is evident that the new part has combined well with the old. It is now a young village; interesting in that the Parish Council have named the new roads after bygone parishioners, ie Parkin Close, Squires Close, Mercia Avenue, Clarks Close, Cooper Close, Hardy's Close, Rawling's Court and Barratt's Close.

Tom Barratt was the boot and shoe repairer, 1894–1986. His work (and sweetshop) was his hobby also, and he was loved by young and old alike. He received Royal Maundy Money from the Queen when she visited Southwell Minster on 19th April 1984.

It's said that Dick Turpin rested in the village in one of the old coaching inns – to be near the lucrative Fosse Way.

The first Old Hall Farm was demolished (a murder, by the footman, is supposed to have taken place there – with ghostly 'happenings' nearby in recent times). The second building with the same name was pulled down to make way for new housing this decade.

The Rev Dobbin had a house built to his own instructions – with underground passages to the church. In the church itself is a long piece of wall plate timber with nail head ornament – this is rare and dates from the 13th century. The belfry contains five bells; two dated 1699 and 1757, the fourth recast in 1905 and the last added the same year.

The Grantham Canal runs through Cropwell Bishop, although now disused and the old bridges taken down to make way for wider roads. The canal was much used to transport night soil, especially from Nottingham. It was thrown onto adjoining fields as manure. Nottingham produced clay pipes at this time and many broken pipes have been found on the banks.

Cropwell Bishop has always been a thriving village. Plaster was mined by Heaseldens and Gotham Plaster Board which provided work for half the men. Cottages were built for the men, but these have now been demolished. The census for 1851 shows that it was then a self-supporting village with a miller, bricklayers, dressmakers, shoemakers, tailors, lace makers, carpenters, a butcher, straw bonnet makers, plumbers etc.

The original Board School is closed as such but is fully used for activities for young people. There is a well supported Methodist chapel and many functions are held in their schoolroom.

In 1932, the Prince of Wales (Edward VIII) came to the village to open the village Memorial Hall – built by men who had fought in the First World War. It is now used by the Women's Institute and other bodies.

Mill Lane had a plaster mill with a fairly tall chimney, which was accidentally demolished by an explosion when the boiler blew up.

Dunham-on-Trent

Dunham-on-Trent is a Trentside village on the Nottinghamshire side of the river. Lincolnshire is on the other side and the two counties are connected by a toll bridge. Running alongside is the water bridge which takes drinking water from Elkesley to Lincoln.

A church with tower was built in the 15th century, but only the tower is now original as the church has twice been rebuilt.

A row of thatched cottages stood at the foot of the bridge, but were replaced by a row of houses in 1911, and named Coronation Terrace as this was the year of the coronation of King George V and Queen Mary.

There are two public houses named The Bridge Inn and The White Swan, and also an antique shop. The well-stocked supermarket is very convenient. Its premises were previously used as a butcher's shop and slaughterhouse. There is also a car and farm machinery repair workshop.

Going out of Dunham on the A57 road the land rises, and on the top stands the new primary school which was officially opened in June 1966. The new vicarage is up there, too, surrounded by trees and undergrowth, which is a haven for birds, rabbits and other small creatures. The old vicarage stands back from the road amid some find old trees, green lawns and flower beds.

51

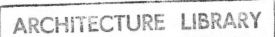
ARCHITECTURE LIBRARY

The old National school, which was built in the early 1840s, stands on a corner by the crossroads. Until it was sold, half was used by the playschool and the other room for table tennis practice. The playschool has been transferred to a large room in the village and the practice teams have moved elsewhere.

Within living memory Dunham has been flooded twice, first in 1910 and again in 1947, when the only means of getting about was by boat. One mother with her new-born baby was rescued through the bedroom window in 1947. All building in the area was banned, but since then, flood banks have been built up to contain the water in the river channel and there have been no more disasters. Permission has now been given for building, and at least 17 new houses have gone up, with plans for more to follow.

East Bridgford 🦢

East Bridgford has never been a sleepy village. It lies on a ridge overlooking a crossing of the river Trent and the busy road to Doncaster and the north. Three quarters of a mile to the east is the ancient Fosse Way (A46) linking Leicester and Lincoln, with evidence of the Roman town of Margidunum nearby.

Between these two strategic highways, villagers must have witnessed at close hand the conflict of the Civil Wars. The local family of Hackers, whose home, the Old Manor is still occupied, were deeply involved on both sides. Indeed Francis Hacker, a staunch Parliamentarian, escorted Charles I to the scaffold and was subsequently executed himself in 1660 after the Restoration. The village is fortunate in having its own history book (*East Bridgford, the Story of a Village*), written by the Rev Du Boulay Hill, rector from 1898–1927, who is still remembered with affection by the older Bridgfordians.

An attractive wooded road leads up the hill from the banks of the Trent to the village crossroads. Occupying a prominent position in the village, the church, standing in its peaceful churchyard, has unspoiled views over the Trent valley with Sherwood Forest in the distance. St Peter's church, dating back 1,100 years, with its long association since the 15th century with Magdalen College, Oxford, is known to have been plundered by the Danes in the 9th century while on their way up the Trent. It was rebuilt almost immediately and has continued as a centre of village life ever since.

Teapot Cottages, East Bridgford

Gypsum was extensively mined in the village over a period of 200 years until 1936. This Satin Spar was of such fine quality that some was exported to North America. At one time six village craftsmen were employed making ornaments. Examples from East Bridgford are exhibited in London museums.

A great tradition of the village is the celebration of St Peter's Day at the end of June. This used to take the form of a week-long holiday and fair, but is now a weekend of village activities known as the Feast Weekend, when friends and families from afar are reunited in the village at the

Horticultural Show on the Saturday. The Royal British Legion and youth organisations participate at the Thanksgiving Service on the Sunday and on the Monday the traditional cricket match is held on the sports field. 1989 was the 125th anniversary of the Flower Show, known to be one of the oldest in England.

The old farmhouses, cottages and barns, built of red brick from the now disused brickyard in the village, are well maintained today. New housing developments have taken place and many of the old orchards have been subject to infill but nevertheless cultivated agricultural land still surrounds the village.

East Bridgford with a population of around 2,000 is a compact lively village. It is a very active community possessing all the necessary amenities needed for today's busy modern life: medical centre, primary school, sports field, post office, six shops including a butcher and general store and two pubs. A Methodist chapel, good village hall and recently rebuilt WI Hall provide attractive meeting places for the activities that give East Bridgford its flourishing community life.

East Drayton

East Drayton is a rural village in the north-east of the county, administered by Bassetlaw District. Retford, the local market town is situated seven miles to the north-west, Newark 17 miles south and Lincoln 15 miles east. The village stands on slightly higher ground than those along the Trent river banks and thus is not liable to flooding.

In 1843 the Tithe Award listed 1,525 acres of arable and pasture land with a small area of woodland. Present day population is about 230 with 74 dwellings; seven active farms remain including a very large arable and a specialist pig farm, others are mixed arable and stock-rearing farms.

Industrial development is restricted to general agricultural engineering and a newly established joinery business using a converted barn.

Up to the opening of the Dunham toll bridge in 1832 the village was situated on the main route from the west to the Trent ferry crossing at Laneham. Happily the main traffic now passes to the south on the A57 trunk road.

A fine 13th century church dominates the village centre, the distinctive tower housing a peal of six bells, regularly rung by the village team of bell-ringers and by visitors.

Also in the village centre is the former school, originally built by the local community in 1861 and now converted by the present villagers for use as a village hall. Local children now travel by bus to the primary school at Dunham and for secondary education to Tuxford.

The old Blue Bell Inn and neighbouring restaurant also stand in the village centre; the latter being on the site of a former smithy.

The village is designated as a conservation area and contains a pleasing mixture of both old and new dwellings, mainly of local red brick with red pantile roofs. Planning restrictions allow small infill development and farm buildings only. The early Victorian vicarage has recently been restored and a former inn dating back at least to the 18th century is under restoration. The village post office, however, is located in part of a modern bungalow.

The Trentside power stations and Rampton Hospital provide most local employment, the numbers in local agriculture being fairly small; other residents commute to surrounding towns daily.

In earlier times a number of different trades allied to agriculture were carried on in the village, which also possessed three windmills and a watermill. Only the sites of these however, remain today.

A notable son of East Drayton was the 17th century architect Nicholas Hawksmoor, a member of an old local farming family. He left the area at the age of 18 to commence his career, during which he worked with Christopher Wren and Vanbrugh on many London buildings including the Royal Naval College, Greenwich. The Farm in which he was brought up was eventually bequeathed to his former step-sister, but its location is uncertain today.

East Leake 🌿

The word 'Leake' is derived from the Anglo-Saxon word 'Lecche', meaning water meadow, and in fact the village lies along the Kingston Brook, a tributary of the river Soar.

Being within easy reach of Nottingham, Leicester and Derby, and also the M1 and East Midlands airport, it has grown considerably. A large council estate was built in the mid-1940s and several housing estates have since been added, making it a popular commuter area.

It still retains its village atmosphere, although it now boasts a library, a health centre and fire station, apart from various shops. The old manor house, built between 1715 and 1728, now houses the post office. There are two junior schools and a comprehensive school (incorporating a leisure centre) which also serves surrounding villages.

The church of St Mary is mentioned in the Domesday Book, when there was a water-mill, three manors and 36 families in the village. It stands on the site of much older buildings and was extensively restored in 1882. A prized possession is the 8 ft Vamp Horn, known in the village as 'the Shawm'. Only five other churches have such an instrument. It was invented in 1670 by Samuel Morland, one of Samuel Pepys' tutors at Cambridge, who called it a 'Tuba Sentorophonica'. Here it was used by the bass singer to lead the choir from the gallery of the church. In 1644 during a local skirmish three Cavaliers and two Roundheads were killed and they lie in unmarked graves near the church porch.

Other denominations are catered for by the Catholic church of Our Lady and the Angels and the Baptist and Methodist chapels, whilst the Evangelical church meets in the village hall. A baptist chapel has existed since 1757, whilst the first Wesleyan chapel was built in 1798, the latter now occupying their third building.

The village green, although not extensive, has a brook running past the war memorial. The remains of the old pound, furnished with seats, now forms a sheltered spot from which to watch the world go by.

Over the years the chief employment has gone from agriculture through knitting and basket making to the present day mining of gypsum. Apart from various types of baskets and furniture, shell cases for use in the First World War were also made from locally grown willows. Some villagers still remember as children, 'stripping the willow'. A recent introduction to local employment is the micropropagation of roses.

The village hall, which celebrated its Golden Jubilee in 1985, was built on land purchased for the purpose by the Women's Institute.

For a number of years there has been an annual tug-of-war across the brook and this has developed into a carnival parade, led by the Youth Band, which has grown out of one of the first Scout and Guide bands in the country.

East Markham

The village of East Markham is situated in north Nottinghamshire on a ridge of high land between the rivers Idle and Trent. The very name suggests a boundary settlement, possibly of the ancient Kingdom of

Mercia. In medieval times the prefix 'East' was usually added, then in Tudor times the 'East' was replaced by 'Great' or 'Much', possibly suggesting it had grown more than West Markham. It reverted to 'East' in 1796 and has been known as that ever since.

During the Middle Ages, East Markham developed into a local market centre but was toppled, not by a rival settlement, but by the outbreak of plague in 1609. One hundred and fifteen deaths were recorded, the last of which was that of the vicar. His own handwriting records 114 deaths, and another unknown hand ends the list with his death. Tuxford then became the market centre and Markham never recovered its importance.

East Markham can claim one or two figures of national importance and the best known was Judge Markham who drew up the Instrument for the deposing of Richard II in favour of Henry Bolingbroke. Another family of importance was the Kirke family who bought Mirfield Hall (now demolished) in 1681. The family remained in the village until 1942 and the Kirke name is perpetuated in house names and, more recently, a street name.

The village green, East Markham

Of all the buildings in East Markham the church stands out as one worth visiting. Nikolaus Pevsner in his book *The Buildings of England* calls it 'the most splendid church in this part of the county'. It has a pleasant setting with a farm on one side and the manor on the other. It contains the alabaster tomb of Judge Markham (d.1409) and a very fine brass (1419), known as the Meryng brass, of Lady Millicent, who was the second wife of Judge Markham. The tomb of the Judge was 'vandalised' in the 17th century by graffiti being scratched on it and this has interested historians. The outline of a coffin and a board game resembling Nine Men's Morris can be easily discerned. The high altar and east window are important early works of Sir Ninian Comper who later became a well-known architect. The other major building in the village is the Hall with its high surrounding wall.

The school was built in 1877 and is still in use. It was built from locally made bricks, which differ in size from modern standard bricks. The local bricks are a deep russet red colour but have a tendency to erode rather badly, thus adding interest to the buildings. There are various patterns in the brickwork of the older houses round the village and one house on Pond Corner has its frontage constructed entirely from 'headers' with no 'stretchers' in sight at all.

Some of the older buildings were and still are farms. One of these is a fruit farm, which continues the tradition of fruit growing in the area. Markham was renowned for its fruit and 'you could always tell when they'd had a good plum crop because the ladies had new bonnets'. Horses and drays queued to get into the local railway sidings to unload their fruit which was then transported by rail to Sheffield, Nottingham and Manchester. It is recorded that in 1886 over 200 tons of plums went by rail from Markham sidings. Apples and pears are the principal fruits now grown commercially in the village.

The problem of protecting the fruit gave rise to 'tenting' (tending) and many children used to stay away from school to 'tent' the fruit and scare away the birds. They also used to go 'cow tenting' down the local lanes. Cow tenting brought danger to the tenters and to the villagers because after a long, dry day in the lanes, the beasts used to stampede back into the village at night to get to one of the two village ponds. Woe betide anyone who got in their way!

The village no longer has a pond although the name Pond Corner still exists. It was on a dangerous bend and a newspaper cutting of February, 1922 reads 'Work has begun on filling in the pond at East Markham. There are few of these old ponds left by the roadside and this one at East

Markham has always been a picturesque feature of the village. . . . . . . In the old days of horse traffic there was no danger . . . [but] . . . recently some impetuous cyclists and chauffeurs have run into the pond'. The bypass now takes the traffic round the village and the dangerous corner has become a cul-de-sac.

East Stoke 🌿

East Stoke has had a long and memorable history, dating right back to the time of the Romans. The Fosse Way which divides the village in two was originally part of the Roman road from Bath to Lincoln. It is believed that the Roman fort of Ad Pontem was sited here.

The manor at Stoke is mentioned in the Domesday Book. The village became known as East Stoke in order to differentiate it from Stoke Bardolf, not as some have argued, to differentiate between the old village which was deserted after the plague and the new village.

East Stoke had its own hospital, which was founded before 1135 by the Ayncourt family of Thurgarton. Being on the site of the present hall it was dedicated to St Leonard. The hospital of St Leonard stood on this site for some 450 years until finally being dissolved in 1573 by Queen Elizabeth I.

In 1487 the last battle of the Wars of the Roses took place at Stoke Field. This was two years after the death of Richard III at Bosworth. The Yorkists were duped into accepting the impostor Lambert Simnel as the rightful heir to the throne. On 16th June of that year, together with 2,000 German mercenaries and 4,000 Irishmen, the Yorkists faced Henry VII's 12,000 men. They nearly won the day but were finally beaten back and in an attempt to escape ran into what is known today as Red Gutter, where many of the 4,000 rebels killed were slaughtered.

The church at East Stoke, dedicated to St Oswald, is of no particular interest save for the fact that the stained glass windows in the chancel and the pointed east window date from the time of Richard II.

There have been several noteworthy citizens of East Stoke. The two most famous are probably Sir Julian Pauncefote, who became the first ambassador to Washington and Thomas Smith who, born in 1631, founded a thriving banking business in Nottingham which in 1902 amalgamated with the Union Bank of London and in 1917 became the National Provincial Bank, Ltd.

Edwalton 🌿

The village is situated three and a half miles from the city of Nottingham, off the A606 Melton road. The name was derived from a Saxon settler named Eadweald who reclaimed land from the marshes.

Although the village has expanded considerably, the main street has managed to keep its village charm. The village field adjoins this street and there are overhanging trees with, in the spring, daffodils lining the road. Farming has now ceased but the farm buildings have been converted into bungalows, which helps to preserve the character of the village. The old school house and the post office still survive alongside the church.

This church was originally built about 1166 and was purported to have been erected by a knight as a penance for his part in the murder of Thomas á Becket. The chancel collapsed in the 17th century and was rebuilt in brick. The tower, however, is believed to be a rare example of building from the time of Mary Tudor. During the 800 year celebrations of the church, two people reported seeing the ghost of a headless woman in the churchyard and in the street.

The remainder of Edwalton consists of four shops, numerous houses, a complex for elderly persons with warden-aided flats, a primary school and a Pentecostal chapel. There is a thriving community with many organisations being attached to the church, which include a drama group which produces a pantomime each year.

Edwinstowe 🌿

Edwinstowe is in the heart of Sherwood Forest and the forest is still a part of village life just as it was in the 7th century.

Edwin, after whom the village is named, was the King of Northumbria. On 12th October, AD 632, Edwin was killed in battle and legend says that Edwinstowe grew up around the church that was built on the spot where his body had rested.

Saxon Edwinstowe remained small. It is recorded in the Domesday Book of 1086 that the population consisted of about 20 people.

Following the Norman Conquest, Edwinstowe came within the bounds of the Royal Hunting Forest of Sherwood, covering about one fifth of Nottinghamshire. The law forbade hunting and the felling of trees and minor offenders were tried at a special court held in the village on a

Friday once every seven weeks and others were tried in Nottingham. In 1334 it is recorded that 119 men were tried for venison trespass and many for taking oak trees.

The parish church of St Mary dates from the 12th century and was the first stone building in the village. Legend has it that Robin Hood and Maid Marion were married here.

During the 16th and 17th centuries the oaks in Sherwood were felled in great numbers to be used for shipbuilding. They were transported to Bawtry by timber drugs and floated down the river Idle to the Trent and the shipbuilding yards at Deptford. Sherwood oaks were also used by the villagers to repair the church after it had been damaged in a thunder-storm in 1672.

In the 18th century the forest was gradually cleared for agriculture and for the parks of the great estates of Rufford, Thoresby, Welbeck and Clipstone. Edwinstowe became part of Welbeck estate and the people were allowed to collect firewood and bracken from the forest and their pigs could be turned out to graze there.

People began to appreciate the beauty of Sherwood Forest at the beginning of the 19th century and droves of trippers travelled the forest roads in horse-drawn brakes and charabancs.

In 1925 sinking work began on Thoresby Colliery and heralded another great change in the appearance and character of the village.

Today Edwinstowe and Sherwood Forest are visited by thousands of tourists from all over the world, anxious to see the Major Oak tree and to hear the legends of Robin Hood and his Merry Men.

Egmanton

Egmanton, in common with many villages, is no longer dependent on agriculture for its survival. Many farmhouses and cottages have been sold to people outside the village but because of this the village thrives. Major housing developments have passed it by and Egmanton remains a pretty, well kept, red brick village with a fine community spirit. Its 1981 population was 196.

The employment structure of the village is varied. There are a number of prosperous farms including Yew Tree Farm (a pig unit) and Manor Farm (a mixed farm). There is a market garden producing exotic pot plants and an agricultural welding business. The main employment

The Old Plough, Egmanton

opportunities within the village are offered by Smiths, who build and repair roads. Egmanton lies above both coal and oil fields and a number of people work for British Coal and British Petroleum. BP's collecting station for the Egmanton oil field is at Ladywood. The East Midlands HQ for BP is at nearby Eakring.

Egmanton lost its primary school and resident vicar in the 1850s and so has to work hard to keep the village together. The village hall is the centre for most activities. The village has a pretty and comfortable pub called the Plough, a post office and a Methodist chapel.

Egmanton attracts many visitors who come mainly to see the church, but who cannot help enjoying the stroll down the village street and seeing the family of ducks on the stream which runs parallel. The church nestles among huge horse chestnut trees with an extensive and noisy rookery. Parts of the church date from the 12th century but it is mainly medieval. It is a lovely stone building, recently re-roofed. The chuchyard is kept tidy by Newark Council but the gravestones remain in their original places (some well-tilted with age). Pilgrims from all over Britain come several times a year to the shrine of Our Lady of Egmanton. This commemorates a vision of the blessed Virgin Mary at Ladywood in early times.

Visitors will also come to see Gaddick Hill, a motte and bailey, behind the church. It was built by William the Conqueror's men for use as a temporary fortress.

Apart from the Stone House on Kirton Road and the church, the village buildings are brick. There are some fine 18th century farm buildings and houses such as North Farm, as well as some imposing Georgian houses like Rotherwood, and more recently Beech Paddocks. The old vicarage has medieval cellars but was rebuilt in late Georgian times with a Victorian facelift. Most houses have large gardens and some have orchards.

Elston 🌿

Elston lies five miles south of Newark and three-quarters of a mile from the Roman Fosse Way. The river Trent is about one and a half miles away and forms the western boundary of the parish. Southwards lies the beautiful Vale of Belvoir and Lincolnshire is within sight to the east. Huge pylons carrying electricity stride across the landscape where hedges have been removed to form large fields.

Finds of Stone Age flint and Roman pottery and coins are evidence of earlier dwellers in the area.

Elston is a compact village developed from two parishes in the form of a rectangle of four roads, Low Street, Top Street, Pinfold Lane and Toad Lane. The church, school, village hall and playing field are within the rectangle. The Hall and all its buildings stand on the south side of Top Street, turned now into modern homes. Within the rectangle there are also developments of modern housing. The barns of a disused farmyard have been converted, with the addition of more houses to form a pleasant development on the south-east corner and the council estate, although outside the rectangle, does not spoil the compactness of the village.

It is a friendly village with good support for local events. There are about 850 inhabitants, most of whom commute to work out of the village. This is a far cry from 150 years ago when there were 13 farmers and most trades had one or two representatives. The local trade of 'skepmaking' (basket making) used willow especially grown in 'rodholts' and stripped by village women and children.

Surrounded as it is by agricultural land, farming continues to be very

63

important although the use of modern machinery has reduced the size of the workforce considerably. There are still a number of working farms in the village.

The village is fortunate to have a post office and general store.

The Hall was owned by the Darwin family from 1680 until 1954. Erasmus Darwin was born here in 1731. He moved to Lichfield after becoming a doctor. He became one of the country's finest physicians, an inventor and founder member of the Lunar Society. His grandson, Charles, is recorded as having said that his theory of evolution owed nothing to Erasmus' work on the subject, which seems uncharitable to say the least!

Another interesting building in the village is the old Elston chapel. The parish of Elston Chapel was created in 1584. The building, with its Norman doorway, has been a puzzle but recent convincing research suggests that the hospital of St Leonard, which was sold in 1576, was in this area and the building could have been the hospital chapel.

Out of the village on the Fosse Way is a recently opened restaurant beautifully restored from the fascinating Victorian Middleton House. Robert Middleton had the building started in 1872. Stories are told that when, on his travels, he saw something he liked he would dash back to Elston to have the particular feature incorporated into his new home. How the builder must have dreaded him appearing with a new idea.

The recently refurbished public house, The Chequers, is the only one left out of three. The other two are now private homes.

Both the church and the Methodist chapel are very fine buildings. There is a modern school and vicarage, replacing the Victorian buildings which are still standing and occupied. The old school has been converted into a private house. The Victorian Darwin Cottages opposite the church replaced the original almshouses provided by Ann Darwin in her will in 1722 and are still occupied by four ladies. The windmill, unfortunately without sails since 1940, has also been converted into a home giving a marvellous view of the surrounding land and of Belvoir Castle.

Epperstone 🌿

Epperstone is one of the most attractive villages in Nottinghamshire. It was granted a conservation order in 1972 and has therefore been protected from speculative development. This, together with a bypass to spare it the ravages of heavy traffic have combined to produce an unspoilt village.

The architecture is varied – old cottages, Georgian and Victorian houses and newer properties built since 1945. A number of houses or part of them date back to the 16th and 17th centuries. The present church is 13th century, apart from the spire and the cock which are a little younger! The altar is an original Communion table which was found in the manor laundry and returned to the church in 1953. The only remaining manor (Epperstone once had three!) was a small 18th century house enlarged during the 19th century. It remained a private residence until the Second World War when the owners lent it to the Red Cross as a convalescent home for wounded soldiers. In 1957 the Nottinghamshire County Constabulary purchased it for their headquarters. On their amalgamation with the City it became and still is a training school for local police forces.

The village school, built in 1855, catered for between 50 and 60 children in the early years of the 20th century, was modernised in the 1960s and closed in 1985.

Four dovecotes are pleasant features of the village. Believed to be about 200 years old, three of them are part of outbuildings attached to the larger houses but the fourth is free standing and as such rather more rare. A pinfold or pound still exists where stray cattle or sheep were penned until claimed.

The Cross Keys is the local hostelry and very popular with locals and visitors.

The population of Epperstone has, with minor fluctuations, changed little over the past 200 years. There are approximately 165 houses including farms in the parish, containing about 460 people.

The present residents take great pride in their properties and gardens – some of which are opened each year under the National Gardens scheme or for local charities.

Until the 1930s, the village was largely self-supporting with most of its wage earners working locally. Apart from the local farms, some of which supplied and delivered milk, eggs and chickens, there was a tanner and tanyard, blacksmith and forge, carter, joiner, cobbler, weaver and tailor. There were two resident butchers who reared and slaughtered their own animals and three or four shops including a post office. Many of the villagers themselves kept a few chickens and during the war, a pig!

Today, Epperstone is mainly a commuter village with little local employment. There is a good post office/general store and papers and milk are delivered daily. A butcher comes twice weekly and a fishmonger/greengrocer once a week.

Socially too, there have been changes. Prior to 1950 the owners of the manor have made available the 'Manor Room', a building attached to the gatehouse. One of the manor fields had also been made available for cricket and this field was most generously donated to the village by Mrs Bourne in 1948 and is the envy of many visiting teams.

When the Manor Room was no longer available, a barn on the cricket field was enlarged into a small village hall and pavilion, but this did not prove to be a satisfactory solution to the needs of the community.

Today there is the Social Institute – a chapel closed for worship in 1900 and taken over by a group of men trustees to provide somewhere for the men of the village to meet and make their own entertainment with billiards, darts, dominoes, skittles etc. This form of socialising was very popular during the days of depression and after the First World War when, in spite of the hardship endured, men missed the companionship they had experienced. With the advent of radio and television these activities fell into decline and the Mens' Institute became the Social Institute and is used today for most village functions.

Everton 🦡

The river Idle meanders in a wide horseshoe from south to north, and across the open eastern end the Chesterfield Canal ensures that Everton is virtually an island. Storms, they say, like witches, cannot cross the water; the more prosaic say that the weather is never extreme because the village lies in a shelter belt.

One of the largest acreages in North Nottinghamshire, Everton is also a lucky village. William Harland Metcalfe, 27th recorded vicar in a line first noted in 1280, resigned the living of Holy Trinity church to become a farmer. When he died in 1944, he left a bequest to the village by means of which the trustees acquired about five acres of recreation grounds, pavilions and the village institute (the old tithe barn).

The village is changing; a few people can list twelve shops in their lifetime, today it is possible to buy guns, antiques and craft items but there is only one general store. Fewer still remember walking through the fields to the ferry across the river Idle. There is no longer an Everton Feast, when stalls were set up on the village green and villagers enjoyed a rare holiday. One custom remains: on Trinity Sunday parishioners make a circle round the church and sing a hymn, 'clipping' (embracing) their spiritual home.

Still to be found are the old malthouse, the former threshing barn, the old brewery and the house where the excise officers stayed when they came to sample the beer. The oldest house still standing dates from the 16th century. Everton, however, has not stood still. It was a group of smallholdings with widely scattered fields; now it is almost a dormitory village. The old centre sits like a bird on her nest, spreading wings that are the modern housing estates on east and west.

Odd things happen in the row of terraced houses that were once the long threshing barn and are now part of the conservation area. There is a ghost of a little dog which is said to scrabble at doors and slip across the hallway in the house where he lived in the early part of the century. A van driver, delivering papers early on dark December mornings, used to see a man walking with a small dog. It seemed unusual but he paid little attention until the morning that he picked them up in his headlights as they vanished through a high brick wall!

Farndon 🌿

Farndon nestles in the Trent valley two miles from Newark along the Fosse Way, and can trace its origins from Roman and Saxon times when it was known as 'Farendune', meaning 'place in the bracken on the bank'.

The church of St Peter, situated in the old part of the village, shows evidence of late Saxon and early Norman foundation – in the remains of a Saxon or Norman plain doorway in the north wall and a section of herringbone walling.

In 1872 it was recorded that 'Farndon is a well built village with a population of 700'. It was also a self-contained village – a merry village – having three pubs, which also organised dances and feasts, and two beerhouses. Three chapels, as well as the church, looked after spiritual needs and the National school provided education for the children, the poorest being paid for by charities.

Farming, malting, willow growing and basket making were the main sources of employment for men and women. There was also the blacksmith, butcher, baker, general stores, and even a cobbler who often worked all night mending boots for many who had only one pair! Pegleg, the roadman, kept the village clean and tidy despite his having only one leg and one stump. He also used his wooden leg as a 'setting-stick' to make holes for potato setting.

Today, Farndon can still boast that 'it is a well built village', even though the population has increased fourfold over the last 40 years,

St Peter's Church, Farndon

which has meant the demolition of many old cottages and buildings to make room for the growth of modern housing. It is a 'garden village', full of lovely trees. There are three shops, one of which has a sub-post office and a newsagency.

Not all of the past is lost. The willows still remain and Mr Lever Howitt, a wealthy and dedicated conservationist, left his estate to the National Trust, so today the Willow Holts (part of Mr Howitt's estate) are being carefully restored and maintained.

In the 1930s sand and gravel was needed to build the aerodrome runways at Syerston and Newton. Excavations on parts of the river bank revealed ample supplies. Today those worked gravel pits have been transformed into a superb marina, the river widened and the marshy fields alongside drained. Though many of the green fields have been used for building houses, there are still many acres left along the banks.

Farndon ferry has played a very large part in the history of the village. In the past the ferryman would be hailed to take passengers across the river. It was easy then to walk to Rolleston to catch a train. Horses and bicycles could also be ferried across – at the owner's risk. Barges carrying coal, grain and other commodities from Hull were a common sight.

It has always been a favourite venue for fishermen and still is, especially as the Britannia Inn stands on the bank overlooking the river. Not so long ago flooding was a hazard. Water might be lapping around, but its customers never had to forego their favourite tipple – the ferryman rowed them into the backyard! One of its landlords even built a dance hall on stilts to avoid the floods and please his customers.

Farnsfield 🌿

There are traces of ancient Roman camps in the village of Farnsfield (or Fernsfield as it was known at the time of the Domesday Book) and it is reputed that the ghost of a Roman soldier has been seen in one of the local hostelries – perhaps the partaking of several spirits resulted in actually seeing one!

It was the birthplace of Augustus Charles Gregory, who emigrated to Australia. He was the first man to explore the interior of the continent and became known as the protector of the Aborigines.

The Southwell Nature Trail and picnic area passes along the north-eastern edge of the village, with an abundance of wildlife, flowers and ferns.

Nearby is Hexgreave Park, the home of Sir John Eastwood, founder of the Sir John Eastwood Foundation which is well known for its charitable work.

With a population of approximately 2,500, Farnsfield is fortunate in having, amongst its many amenities, a church, chapel, library, bank, chemist, post office and four public houses. A walk down Main Street brings one to a wide variety of other shops, including a baker's, hairdresser's, supermarkets, etc.

One of the latest attractions to the village has been the introduction of a Modern Farm which has brought many visitors, especially coachloads of children, to see a wide variety of interesting and unusual animals.

A few years ago the church, in a bid to raise money for repairs, instituted a May Day Market which necessitated the closing of Main Street to traffic and the erection of market stalls. Attractions included brass bands, strolling minstrels, Punch and Judy show and a miniature railway. Thousands of people visited the fair and after several very successful years, the running of the fair has been taken over by the Farnsfield Young Peoples Trust.

November brings the Remembrance Day Parade and service arranged by the local branch of the Royal British Legion, after which a large congregation gathers outside the church to witness the laying of the wreaths at the foot of the stone cross which records the names of the men from Farnsfield who fell in the two World Wars.

In the churchyard is the tomb of Sarah Burgess, who died in 1823. She lived in style in a large Georgian house in the village and it is said that this was a grace and favour house given to her by King George III.

The Farnsfield and District Horticultural Society, which also incorporates the villages of Kirklington and Edingley, hold various talks on gardening, flower shows, a garden party and a barbecue, all efforts culminating in a mammoth Horticultural Show in August. The main marquee is a sight to behold with the biggest and best flowers, fruit and vegetables that months of hard work can produce.

Fiskerton ✤

On rounding the bend on the road from Rolleston to Fiskerton, one is greeted by the river Trent to one's left; a gently curving river bordered by meadows and trees. The river stretches into the distance and one can see

70

on the right the old wharf and Bromley Arms pub, both still used by the river traffic – a picture of serene beauty and tranquillity.

Just three miles from Southwell, Fiskerton was a fairly industrial village in the mid-19th century. It had a lace thread factory and a firm making blacking, ink and stove polish; whilst to cope with the then extensive river trade there were several wharves, warehouses and maltings. The river Trent played an important part in the then prosperity of Fiskerton with the barges plying their passage upstream from Hull and Goole to Nottingham. Today it is a popular watering hole for the leisure craft who use the river. This area is often put to good use as the village square, where special village markets are held and one regularly hears the jingle of bells indicating that the morris men are busy entertaining again. What is not generally known, however, and is unusual for the size of the village, was that in 1270 Henry III's charter granted a weekly market to Fiskerton and, what meant far more, a fair on the feast of Holy Trinity.

The observant traveller will notice the many levelled grassy areas close to the river's edge, for this stretch of the river Trent is very popular with fishermen, who come from miles around to what is reputed to be one of the finest fishing stretches on the Trent. Many fishing competitions take place here, but it's not just the fishermen who compete for the fish. Round one of the river's bends is a heronry and a heron in flight is a regular sighting. The beautiful blue of the kingfisher is often seen too, amongst the other river wildlife abounding in this beautiful area.

Far less tranquil times were experienced, however, according to the history books, for it was at Fiskerton (reputedly at the Bromley Arms) that the troops who had marched from Southwell, crossed the Trent to East Stoke in 1487 for the final battle of the Wars of the Roses. The number of those killed varies but records state that on the marshy ground (still marked on the Ordnance Survey map as the 'Gutter) at Fiskerton the carnage was so great that the Trent ran red with blood.

These days the battle is more likely to be played on the cricket field or skittling in the Bromley Arms – a pub certainly in existence in 1844. Although many new executive style houses have been built to cater for the increasing demand for homes in this lovely area, they blend well with the character of the village. The local railway station is not only used by the villagers but also by the sporting public, for Southwell racecourse is on the border between Fiskerton and the neighbouring village of Rolleston.

Flawborough 🌿

This is a delightful small village away from the main traffic routes and in the spring the daffodils in the area of the church are a joy.

The church was rebuilt in 1840 of red brick. It stands in an area of the village from which a good view of the countryside is obtained. One can see over the river Smite to Thoroton, Sibthorpe with its dovecote and Shelton, Cotham and Elston. From the other side may be seen Belvoir Castle and Bottesford church spire. The land is farmed, with just one edge of the village mined for gypsum.

Flintham 🌿

If you were to stand in the middle of the village, holding picture postcards of the Main Street taken in the early 20th century you would see hardly any difference between now and the views on the cards. The buildings are identical, warm brick and pantile; a tree has matured, making a pleasant street even more attractive and opposite it, tucked in by the shop, there is an old red phone box. Little has changed the character of the Main Street over the years.

And yet – there's one vital difference between today's view and the postcards. The postcards show people going about their business, children permanently captured, standing in the middle of the road looking inquisitively towards the photographer; a bread van with a horse waiting patiently for his owner. Today, more often than not there will be nobody about.

When the photographer set up his camera all those years ago, Flintham Hall still owned a high proportion of the cottages and employed many villagers in some capacity on the estate. Gradually, cottages have been sold and the families dependent on the estate do not now reach double figures.

The shop opposite the mature tree still looks 'shop-like' at a quick glance, but it closed in the early 1980s. What a treasure trove of memories were revealed at the back of the shelves when they were cleared for the last time. Mazawattee tea, piano wires, pre-war Valentine cards jostled with medicines guaranteed to relieve every illness known to man and horse. At about the same time, the mobile grocery van stopped, ending a family link with the bread cart on the postcards. Suddenly, from being a reasonably self-sufficient village there was nothing left. All the shops and businesses run in the village had gone.

But not all is lost as some aspects of village life have perhaps improved. The village school is still alive, a busy hive of activity. Membership of the WI, founded in the 1920s, is growing again; a Youth Club has started; there are various uniformed groups for the younger boys. There is the possibility of using the old school hall during weekdays for village use rather than for school use. The congregations at the church are increasing, although the chapel continues to decline. The pub is busier and regular wine evenings are held in the old school hall. The Flintham Village Newsletter, started in the 1980s, continues to thrive and grow.

Gamston & Bassingfield

Gamston and Bassingfield were really two tiny hamlets (total population just over 100 before the Second World War) with a little lane connecting the two places. There were five farms in Gamston and four in Bassingfield and all the local people worked on the farms producing milk, eggs, fat cattle and pigs along with crops. One of the fields was reputed to be a burial ground, and there is an Iron Age/Roman site under one field waiting to be explored.

There was once a village green with a pump where every householder had to get their own water, there was no street lighting and gas was not introduced until 1930. A Victorian letter box still stands.

All the village life revolved around the farms. Harvest Supper was a big affair when a barn would be cleaned and whitewashed for the occasion. Ham, sides of pork and barrels of beer would be given by the farmers for this, the wives doing all the baking. One character who is remembered as Peg Leg because of his wooden leg, cycled every day from Nottingham to do a full day's work on the farm. A farmer who was well known as quite a gent when out, would lapse into his native tongue on the farm – a favourite expression of his was, 'Gie them 'osses some watter'. It is unbelievable the amount of work that would be done in those early days. Ten-acre fields were ploughed by one man and two horses. Potato setting and picking was all done by hand and then the same person would milk the cows by hand after a day in the fields.

It has been sad to see the disappearance of farms and green fields in the last few years. A busy main road now divides Gamston and Bassingfield and if you are travelling by car you have to negotiate two main roads to reach Bassingfield. There are no farms in Gamston at all now and only two in Bassingfield.

Mobile home sites have added to the population, now standing at 170. The Village Institute has been renovated over the years and has witnessed three moves in its lifetime. It has been the focal point in the village for dances and whist drives.

The old main road was a mere track in the old days, with its humpback bridge over the canal and what a thrill it was to leave the car seat for a second as you bumped over it! This A52 has become a very busy main road and thriving businesses have grown beside it. People come from far and near looking for dogs at Gamston Kennels and Gamston Produce has become quite big and now has a frozen meat shop. There are now two sets of traffic lights in the short distance between the bridge and Gamston Lane and this heralds great changes indeed.

As the last apples were being picked in the autumn of 1988, bulldozers and earth removers rolled up Gamston Lane. The building project proposes to erect 1,800 houses, schools, shops, community centre and a pub, also a main road to Edwalton. Sleepy Gamston will become 'Spring Meadows' and it will become an extension of West Bridgford with its 30,000 inhabitants.

Gamston, Eaton & Rockley

These three small villages are connected by the river Idle. Before 1066 there were two mills and two manors at Gamston, since then it has been part of the Duke of Newcastle's estate.

In 1782 there was a candlewick manufactory, one of the first of its type in the world. It employed 100 hands working in relays night and day, and the weekly wage bill was £400, a considerable amount in those days. This was demolished in 1854.

In the 19th century there was a corn mill and a cotton mill, the latter being near the river bridge. The calico was spread on the meadows to bleach in the sun. This mill was abandoned in 1837 and afterwards used as a flour mill.

The church of St Peter is mainly a 15th century building, but the nave, arcade and chancel arch are 13th century. The Perpendicular tower is 120 feet high and houses a very fine peal of six bells.

The Church of England school was founded in 1856 with 56 pupils.

The building has been extended and the living accommodation which was for the headteacher has been incorporated into the school. Gamston House, part of which was originally the old rectory, is now a private preparatory school.

The Reverend Dan Taylor, founder of the General Baptist New Connexion was baptised in the river Idle by Joseph Jeffery in 1763 and a Baptist chapel, built on the site of the original meeting house, was dedicated to Rev Taylor in Sept 1880. Unfortunately this no longer exists.

There is now no village shop or post office or inn, and there are between 300 and 350 inhabitants and a mixture of new and old houses.

Eaton is a small hamlet, which has a Hall which in 1919 was bought from the Duke of Newcastle's estate by Mr Charles Kayser. During the Second World War the Hall was used as a Maternity Hospital for servicemen's wives and then was extended and became a Teacher Training College. This closed in 1979 and is now Eaton Hall International and used by Notts County Council as a conference centre. The church was largely rebuilt in 1860, and the former village school is now a private dwelling.

Rockley is a small hamlet with an old water mill called Jacket Mill, now a private dwelling. However the village was once famous for its eels – in 1826 in a single night after a thunderstorm, 57 stones of eels were caught. London fishmongers were always wanting eels from the river Idle.

Rockley Methodist chapel was founded in 1827 and is still in use today. Of 13 cottages in Mill Lane at that time, five were occupied by chairmakers' families who were staunch Methodists. Two of these men – Mr Walker and Mr Nicholson – stamped their names on to the edge of the Windsor chair seats, so enabling them to be identified as examples of their work. Some of these are in the Lincoln Museum of Bygone Days. Mr Wheatland was another such furniture maker who instigated the building of the chapel.

Gedling ❧

It is difficult in the present suburban spread to find traces of 'The site at the mouth of a pleasantly situated valley, Ousedyke in the Vale of Trent where Ghellinge stood'. But the area around the 13th century church is still thought of as the village.

William Peveril (tradition says he was William the Conqueror's bastard son) built the first Nottingham Castle and he was given 10 acres of land to make an orchard in Ghellinge. It survived to within living memory just below the church on Grimm Lane (Jessops Lane). In 1279 King Edward gave money to buy eight does and four buck to be taken from Sherwood Forest at Ghellinge, to stock Colwick Park.

Church life was part of all life in the village, and from Anglo-Saxon times, it was not only used for services but as a communal hall where miracle and pastoral plays were performed. What a wonderful day for the locals when the new church, being built from locally quarried stone, began to rise on the hill. In 1587 there was a vicar and a rector in Ghellinge, not easy with only one church, and during one land disagreement the Archbishop of York had to intervene and calm things down. People at this time worked on farms, in the two manor houses, the mills and fishery. There was a hop garden in Waverley Avenue and a workhouse at the top of Stoke Lane. The kennels on Lambley Lane had a huntsman in charge and Dovecote Farm tells its own story. Church records began in 1588 and many names from then survive locally today.

In 1853 White's Directories show Gedling to have a rural population including two Lady farmers, three shoemakers, a tailor, dressmaker, gamekeeper, gardener, builder and blacksmith (this job being done in 1853 by Mary Skellington and in 1869 by Ann Skellington.) The rectory was built in 1702 and the rector usually at this time was a man of means. All Hallows school was built opposite the rectory in 1814. The fountain given by the Countess of Carnarvon of Gedling Manor in 1874 was on the triangular village green.

Some coal was found locally during the Middle Ages and transported on the Trent, but sinking for coal began in 1898 when two shafts 18 feet in diameter were sunk in Bell field (where the church bells had been cast) in 1900. This and the coming of the railway in 1846 began the changes which made the village into a suburb of Nottingham. A few old houses remain, the dovecote, Manor Farm (reputed to have the ghost of a young girl) the fountain, two manor houses and All Hallows school, the church and churchyard, with the graves of Shaw and Shrewsbury, famous cricketers said to be buried a cricket pitch length apart, but in fact rather farther apart than this.

Girton ✧

Girton ('gravel farm') straddles the A1133. The newer half has developed along the pleasant tree-lined New Lane to the east, because the older part lies in the washlands of the Trent, and until recently was regularly flooded. (Then it was said that the people of Girton had webbed feet.) Legend says that one night as the villagers huddled in their upstairs rooms, the church bell began to toll eerily across the flood waters. Next morning it was found that cattle had moved to the highest ground and into the church, and had been chewing at the straw bell rope. But there has been no flood since 1977 when a boat moored at the church gate was used to ferry villagers (and the poor dogs!) to the main road, and row children to their school at Besthorpe. A floodstone on the wall of Chantry cottage marks the highest floods since 1852.

The church, dedicated to St Cecilia, was rebuilt in 1876 on the site of an older building. There is a late 8th century cross worked on a stone to the right of the door. This is the oldest ecclesiastical artefact in the diocese of Southwell. The church has a fine new set of kneelers worked by villagers and friends.

Brick walls with rounded toppings are a feature of the old village, where the village hall sits among the 19 brick and usually pantiled houses, and is used occasionally – most notably for the Harvest Supper when it is filled to capacity for the biggest village event of the year.

Village industries include farming and haulage, gravel extraction, egg production, tripe dressing, kennels and catteries, and the power stations along the Trent provide employment for some, though many people work further afield.

The gravel working left a lagoon which was landscaped and is now used for sailing, and the river Fleet opens into a lake to the south, enjoyed by fishermen and bird watchers, where a variety of wild life includes herons.

Gotham ✧

'Tell me no more of Gotham fools,
Or of their eels in little pools,
Which they were told were drowning;

77

Nor of their carts drawn up on high
When King John's men were standing by,
To keep a wood from burning.'

Looking out from the school building in Kegworth Road, completed in 1880 to replace the old school used since 1829 – is that pond in the opposite field where the ancient Wise Men tried to drown an eel? Beyond in the distance is Cuckoo Bush mound, where the 'Gotham fools' are said to have built a fence round a cuckoo.

On Court Hill, many men from Saxon to medieval times must have assembled to dispense justice and administer the affairs of the villages of the Hundred of Rushcliffe. In the same location may lie the long since vanished site of Rushcliffe Hall; home of the St Andrewe family whose last male heir died in 1625. Splendid alabaster tablets in the 12th century church of St Lawrence commemorate the family's existence.

The early rooks, symbols of past generations, flap around the church spire. In one of its shadows is the imposing Regency facade of the rectory. In another shadow the manor house stands firm. What a wealth of tales must lie within the more ancient of its beams. Nearby in the village centre the Sun hostelry waits quietly. Perhaps in its heyday it was a coaching inn when the old road from Nottingham to the south passed through the village before 1739.

Between the Sun and the church wall stands one of the village pumps. Earl Howe, in the early part of the 19th century, caused water to be conveyed by pipes from Weldon Hill. Ann Seward, the poetess, paying a visit to the old rectory in 1767 wrote:

'At four, we resume my aunt's apartment. Its large and lightsome window commands, it is true, no other prospect than the church-yard over the garden wall, and the village below, which is broad and grassy, with thinly scattered houses. Now, in the latter end of August, the evening spectacle from seven to eight, is truly pleasing and joyous. A majestic old elm stands in the middle of the green-sward, circled round by a mossy seat and is the rendezvous of the village youths and maidens, when the labours of the day are past. Some of the young men wrestle; some play at quoits; and others sit on the bench and talk to the lasses. It is impossible to express the satisfaction I have in beholding these natural and innocent pleasures – "scene of athletic sports and whisper'd vows".'

It is a view of a lost world, when Gotham was a self-sufficient community. All year round, weather permitting, the carrier's cart travelled to Nottingham on Wednesdays and Saturdays. Otherwise, most of life's needs were catered for in the community. Postal and money order services could be obtained. Butchers, bakers and grocers were in business. There were skilled craftspeople such as saddlers, a shoemaker, a dressmaker, a tailor, a joiner and a brickmaker. There were also a few framework knitters in the cottages on Bag Lane. The year followed a pattern, framed by the land and the seasons.

Granby ✖

The village of Granby is situated in the Vale of Belvoir, within easy reach of Nottingham, Grantham, Newark and Melton Mowbray thus making it an ideal place for commuters seeking work in any of these towns. Many of the residents though are involved in mixed farming. Up to date machinery, equipment and methods have eased the life of working on the land in many aspects but in spite of this, the human touch still plays an important part. It is not an uncommon sight for an orphaned lamb to be seen in a box in a farmhouse kitchen, being bottle-fed by the lady of the house. The weather remains a dominant feature too, for during harvest an inclement forecast necessitates workers using the combine harvester long after dark with the aid of headlights. Not 'making the hay while the sun shines' but reaping before the rains come. People who work outside the village are engaged in many and varied occupations such as medicine, education, trade, commerce and industry.

Over the years Granby has seen many changes. Within the last hundred years the population has decreased from around 500 to under 300. One contributory factor to this fall is that many of the old two-up two-down cottages in which large families were once reared have been combined to make one very attractive modernised home of today. Even with the building of new houses, inevitable in most villages, the drop in population cannot be recouped.

The post office is the sole survivor of numerous shops. At one time there were no fewer than five tailors and five shoe repairers plying their trade, along with all the usual suppliers and cottage industries necessary to keep the inhabitants of the village self-sufficient.

The centre of the village is dominated by the towered church, as it has been over many centuries. The building, much restored over the years, is dedicated to All Saints and like many other village churches is one of a group known as the Wiverton group of parishes. Worshippers have, no doubt, visited the site for many years, as suggested by the fact that a Roman altar was dug up in the churchyard in 1812. Probably Granby was situated on one of the roads linking Roman stations such as those in the Bingham and Bottesford areas.

Close by the church is the village hall, which once housed the local school until the reduction in the number of pupils forced its closure and the children were transferred to a neighbouring village school. Today the hall serves as a centre for the leisure activities of both young and old alike. At one time many clubs would have met in the chapel schoolroom for social events as well as for religious classes. There has been a Wesleyan chapel in Granby since 1807.

One of the village's two public houses – the Marquis of Granby, stands as a reminder that Granby was 'remarkable for giving the title of Marquis to the Duke of Rutland whose ancestor purchased the estate. . . . . .' (from White's History, Gazetteer & Directory of Nottingham 1853). A fact of which Granby is very proud.

Greasley

Greasley, formerly Griseleia, was mentioned in the Domesday Book as possessing a church and a priest, but it does not follow the usual pattern of country villages. There is no village green, no duckpond and no snug cottages clustered around its church, but it is still very pleasant with attractive cottages, houses, farmlands and woods.

Little was known of Greasley until the 14th century when Nicholas de Cantelupe was granted royal permission to fortify his manor house adjoining the church and it became Greasley Castle. Traces of the moat and walls remain at the existing Castle Farm.

In 1345 Nicholas founded a Carthusian priory. After the Dissolution of the Monasteries the priory quickly deteriorated – many a farm building was built or repaired from its stones. An altar stone was uncovered in a local farmyard and lovely medieval stained glass roundels can be seen in windows in the church.

Every year in May, the clergy in their robes and the congregation carrying banners walk in procession from the local Roman Catholic church to hold a service at the ruins of the priory.

The church of St Mary stands on a slope where churches have been for a thousand years. There is a list of rectors spanning hundreds of years. In the parish record of 1603 is the marriage of John Robinson, who was pastor to the Pilgrim Fathers and gave the farewell message to them in Leyden before they sailed in the *Mayflower*.

In 1662 a chapel was built in Moorgreen, according to Baron von Hube, on the site of a barn where divine worship had been held. The first priest was the Rev Smalley of Greasley, and at this time of religious conflict it took courage to worship away from the parish church, so that the chapel resembled a house set among tall trees. Services are still held there today.

The priory ruins at Greasley

Deep in High Park Woods stands the imposing Beauvale House built by Earl Cowper, with a tall turreted tower on one side demanded by his wife, who is said to have wished to survey her domains.

Moorgreen reservoir lies at the end of the road winding through the village – very lovely with woods around it and built originally to feed the Nottingham Canal.

Lamb Close House looks over the water, built in 1753 by Matthew Lamb, a coal owner. Sea coal, as it was called, was known even to the monks and small 'bell pits' were dug in many places, but with the discovery of rich deep seams life changed for the community and the countryside.

Small children worked in the mines and in 1756 the Rolleston family of Watnall founded Bog End school in a cottage near the church to help these children who were too weary to learn after work. Sir Lancelot Rolleston and the Rev Mansell, vicar of Greasley, gave land and money to set up a trust to provide money at Christmas for scholars who attended full time. This trust still makes an annual gift to scholars today, and the cottage at Bog End is still occupied.

Dick's Lane, a public footpath by the side of the old bakehouse, runs down a steep slope of fields to the next village in the valley. Before Brinsley owned a church, burials had to be in Greasley churchyard and bodies were borne along roads and up the hillsides with coffin rests at various stages. At that time it was called Coffin Lane.

In the past few years, with the closure of the pits and the grassing over of the pit hills, Greasley has lost its tradespeople. With just one inn and a flourishing garden centre, many residents now are professional people, although the farming community remains important.

Now the threat of open cast mining hangs over the area like a dark cloud and local people are involved actively in the prevention of this desecration, being anxious to preserve the landscape called by D. H. Lawrence, 'The country of my heart'.

Gringley on the Hill

An altitude of 82 feet is not high, but the sudden drop away to sea-level on the north side leaves Gringley quite definitely 'on the Hill', while to the south-west the next high spot is Lincoln, 25 miles away. Beacon Hill itself is a mystery. In spite of several investigative digs, no-one can say for certain whether it is man-made or not. It has been used for many things –

beacon fires (of course), the latest for Armada '88, and at least once for roasting an ox, though in 1933 this brought vegetarians out in protest! In the 1920s and 1930s it was a favourite spot with radio enthusiasts. Now, each year on Rogation Monday a procession climbs to the top to ask God's blessing on all around.

The village church of St Peter and St Paul is 12th century with a later tower and aisles, and has four bells, recently tuned and hung in a new steel frame. The old oak frame is still in position at the top of the tower. Oddly, one bell is dated during the Commonwealth period when the general trend was to dispense with such items, which were thought frivolous. Account books show that the church was holding (illegal) Christmas communion services then, too.

Part of one former Methodist chapel has become a house, but the other is still flourishing as a place of worship.

The shaft of a butter cross stands near the church – a great hazard for drivers in the early days. They suggested breaking it up for road building after it was twice involved in collisions, but commonsense prevailed and it must have learnt its lesson – it hasn't collided with anything since the increasing seaside traffic started using the new bypass!

This is the A631 which runs between Bawtry (in Yorkshire) and Gainsborough (in Lincolnshire), cutting off the rest of Nottinghamshire to the south. And the northern boundary is the river Idle about three miles away across what was swamp before Dutch engineers drained it for farmland in the 17th century.

The older houses are built of bricks made in the old brickworks down by the Chesterfield Canal. Quite a few have tumbled gables and there is a sprinkling of dovecotes. Only a sprinkling of new housing too, as Gringley is a conservation area, so the population has stayed around 650 for a very long time. Until 1956 one large house was in use as a Children's Orthopaedic Hospital – the bracing air of Gringley was felt to be of particular benefit to TB sufferers.

The school, built in 1855, is St Peter's Church of England aided primary school, with a steadily rising number on roll. One of the earlier headmasters wrote a maths textbook, encouraged by the eccentric vicar, Gustavus Hopton Scott. He was a great one for going to law (he always appeared on his own behalf) and would never accept that when the new diocese of Southwell was formed in 1884 his legal obligation was now to that bishop and not the bishop of Lincoln. He did not believe in diocesan interference anyway and saw off all officials with a shotgun. When he died in 1910 after 53 years in the parish, the church was falling into ruin.

Fortunately his successor had an architect brother and they managed not only to save the building but to add a whole new aisle, a tremendous feat for a congregation of small farmers and tradesmen.

Nowadays the population, while still including farmers, has a large proportion of professional people who commute daily. J. H. Rennison, engineers and C. & M. Rennison, builders and decorators are two local firms, and the Brynmill Press publishes books and periodicals. The post office and the newsagents are both also general stores, fresh fish and meat come in mobile shops and of course there is the library van, so the village is still almost self-sufficient.

Grove ✍

Grove is a very small village lying just to the east of Retford. A Roman habitation existed in the moat field surrounded by Castle Hill Woods. The woods now cover only 70 acres but in days gone by they covered a much larger area. The monks from Worksop Priory had the right to collect firewood from the woods to use for cooking and for heating their chambers.

The 'Private Walk' was exactly that. When the Harcourt-Vernons lived in Grove Hall the lady of the house, often being pregnant, liked to walk in privacy so a hard path was laid from the Hall up into the woods. Flowering shrubs were planted along the path. At the far end of the path monkey puzzle trees still grow.

Spring arrived in the village with posies of primroses collected for Mothering Sunday from Coney Green pond, followed by violets, cowslips and later bluebells. The only warning local children were given about going into the woods was 'make plenty of noise if you hear shooters'.

Being a farming community, an important event on the social calendar was the harvest festival. A choir would come from Retford and afterwards all the children ran from church to the Hall where refreshments were served. There was also a Sunday school and of course the Sunday school outing.

Mr Parkin was churchwarden. He rang the bells, wound the clock, took the collection and lit the boiler. He also made the children giggle because his shoes squeaked as he walked up the aisle. As the church was very cold, one of the children in the congregation in those days, remembers the bright idea of hot water bottles. They hung them round their necks under their coats. Unfortunately one day a string broke and it finished with a splash on the stone floor.

Grove is on a hill, so in winter there were plenty of good sledging runs and there was skating on the moat – which had to be tested by one of the fathers jumping up and down. They never lost one!

Mr Yelland was a local character who had been the joiner at the Hall until it was sold and the village children were always sure of a warm welcome round the stove in his workshop. They would sit many hours listening to his tales of Devon and the First World War. In the 1950s there was a blacksmith in the village who would shoe the horses and repair any metal implements. Also about this time travelling shops supplied the villagers with essentials.

Some people would say Grove has not changed over the years. Most of the houses are still there. There is a garden centre and reservoir, but the almshouses are uninhabitable now. There have been a few new houses and farm building conversions. The joiner's shop has been pulled down. The blacksmith died and the business ceased. The Sunday school finished many years ago.

Gunthorpe ✺

Gunthorpe, a small village on the north side of the river Trent, approximately halfway between Nottingham and Newark, probably owes its existence to the fact that the river was fordable at this point. In the first century AD the Romans from the fort of Margidunum on the Fosse Way, made use of this ford on their journeys to and from the lead mines in Derbyshire. It was here that the famous British Queen Boadicea with her tribesmen defeated the Roman Tenth Legion in a fierce battle.

The manor of Gunthorpe is recorded in the Domesday Book, having been given by the Conqueror to one of his nobles, Roger de Busli, who held many manors in this region. No church was recorded in Domesday, but at a later date there are records of the ancient 'Chappell of St James', a chapel of ease of the parish church of Lowdham. This church was allowed to fall into disrepair, and for more than a hundred years, Gunthorpe had no church of its own. The present church of St John the Baptist was built in 1850 by the vicar, the Rev J. H. Browne, who also in 1873 built the old school by the riverside.

During the 19th century the village, which had been mainly agricultural, adopted the trade of framework knitting. This provided a living for many families who hired machines to work in their own homes. These machines were producing underwear until the First World War. There were still a few machines in operation in the parish in the 1930s.

The building of a railway line in the 1840s, with a station at Lowdham, gave many villagers the opportunity of travelling to work in the factories in Nottingham. There was also improved access to the south. It had only been possible to cross the river by means of a ferry boat, but this service was liable to be disrupted in bad weather and at times of flood. A toll bridge was built in 1875 and it proved a great success. But with the advent of motor traffic, even this bridge became inadequate. In 1927 the present bridge was opened.

Walking through the village today, the visitor will find very few obvious traces of the past. The Victorian church is still there. The interior has been modernised, and the beautiful warm colours of the sandstone show up well in the recently installed floodlighting. The old village post office and general stores has been replaced by more modern and spacious premises, but is still being run by the same family. Many of the really old cottages have long since been pulled down and replaced by modern housing. On the riverside, downstream of the bridge, the old toll house still stands tall, now in use as a restaurant. The Victorian school building by the river is also a restaurant. A new Church of England school has been built in David's Lane. Immediately after the Second World War the village set about the daunting task of raising enough money to build a village hall with adjoining playing fields. This has proved a valuable amenity, much used by the community.

The coarse fishing season attracts fishermen from far and wide, and water skiing is a popular attraction at Gunthorpe. Since the building of the Colwick sluices, there is little danger of the serious flooding which used to occur when the river was very high.

Halam 🌿

At the beginning of the 20th century, if you stood at the top of Halam hill and looked down over the village, you would have seen acres of orchards and flower-filled green lanes and verges. This has changed, as has so much in this tiny picturesque place. Halam is an ancient village, mentioned in 10th century ecclesiastical records – it has been suggested that the name is of Anglo-Saxon origin meaning hidden or secret valley.

The church, dedicated to St Michael the Archangel, is of Norman foundation, a chantry chapel of Southwell Minster. Local tradition has it that the stones from which the church was built were 'removed' from carts hauling loads of stone to Southwell to construct the Minster. The carts waited at the foot of Halam hill, which then of course was considerably steeper than now, to await extra horses for additional pulling power. In the 16th century the inhabitants of Halam petitioned the Minster for permission to bury their dead within the village owing to the perils and dangers of the journey to Southwell from robbers and vagabonds. The dovecote is also of Norman origin, all that is left of the early manor house.

Until the 1980s this was a village with a largely elderly population where little had changed for many years. The collective memory goes back over a hundred years to a time when the community was almost entirely self-sufficient. There is still a mill, post office, shop and pubs but the other trades such as blacksmith, cobbler/shoemaker, butcher, hemp and flax workers, cordwainers, carpenter and wheelwright have disappeared, as have the osier beds and rush/flax fields along with the dams that controlled the water flow to them. A resident, now 100 years old, can clearly remember as a girl walking to Kirklington on quarter days to take her father's tithes to the rector. Another elderly resident speaks of the Rev Smith who, at the turn of the century, walked to Halam three times each Sunday to take the services.

The focus of village life today is centred on church and WI activities and on the well-attended village school. As there is no village hall the school premises double as a meeting place.

Halam, although no longer surrounded by orchards, is still an enchanting and fascinating place.

Halloughton 🦎

The village church at Halloughton was restored in the late 1800s as the original medieval building had fallen into a state of disrepair. There are some very early gravestones still readable. Of considerable interest to historians of the medieval era is the one marking the grave of Sir Frank and Lady Doris Stenton. Frank Merry Stenton was Professor of Modern History and later Vice-Chancellor of Reading University where his wife was also a lecturer. Sir Frank was the author of *Anglo-Saxon England* in the Oxford History of England series. His wife was responsible for writing the book *English Society in the Middle Ages*, an insight into life in England after 1066.

If you look at the gravestone attributed to one Elizabeth Tongue, who departed this life in 1819, you will see the stonemason went by the name of Nicholson, but what about the markings under his name – a plant in a pot – an urn – a gravestone! Were these the doodlings of Mr Nicholson?

Halloughton Manor Farm is a most interesting building and although it is now a private residence, must have an intriguing history. At one end of what appears to be a straightforward 18th century farmhouse is a tower – with windows. Not unlike a small castle it would have been a defended house or tower house with no obvious means of access from the ground floor to the two upper floors. Halloughton (pronounced Halorton) came under the jurisdiction of Southwell Minster and under the direct control of the Archbishop of York and in the 14th century, when this was built, it was prudent to build something which could be easily defended. These days invading armies would have a job to find the village, as it lies just off the A612 between Lowdham and Southwell.

Harworth & Bircotes 🦎

The twin villages are in the northernmost part of the county. Harworth is a village which dates back to Saxon times, but it was not until the years before the First World War, when coal was discovered nearby that the mining village of Bircotes was envisaged.

The village is unique in its conception because it was designed with wide streets with curves and crescents, in contrast to the regular pattern of mining villages. The sturdily built houses soon became homes for the incoming miners from Yorkshire, Lancashire and Northumberland. New traditions and accents came too, some of which survive to the present day. The gradual intermingling of rural and mining communities has established a unity of friendly caring people; this spirit is known throughout the county.

The sale of the colliery houses has given rise to a new spirit of pride in the dwellings. Over a thousand houses are now under private ownership and this has given the old colliery homes a new facelift. Until recently Harworth retained its rural image, but with the building of a new estate on Common Lane, also a new church hall, the increase in population has brought new life and purpose to it.

Sadly the shops in the villages have not kept pace and the lack of

Harworth Colliery

grocery shops sends the populace out of the villages to the nearby towns. So the wheel turns full circle and minds are cast back to the times of 'Big fat Charlie'. This was the name of the charabanc which took the villagers to do their shopping in the early days of the mining village.

> 'Clear the way for Big fat Charlie
> Whiskers like a field of barley
> Clear the way for Big fat Charlie
> Coming down the lane'

This song was sung when the people travelled on the wide charabancs.

The connections with the Galway family of nearby Serlby Hall are reflected in the naming of the streets of Bircotes. Monckton is the family name of the Galways and Monckton Road is named thus, other names of the family and friends have also been included. At Harworth crossroads is a cruck cottage which was used by Lady Galway for a hospital in the First World War. Another connection with the Serlby estate is Brailsford House, which was endowed as a school for the children of Harworth. At the present time it has been converted into a residential home for the elderly.

Present life revolves around the colliery and the later industries which came along. The glass bulbs factory commenced work in 1950 and the shoe factory a little later. Two small industrial estates, one at Plumtree and one on the Blyth road, add to employment opportunities.

Sport and music have always had a dedicated following in the villages. Memorable were the pre-war gala days which attracted sportsmen and women of national and international fame. The cups and trophies on show in Milnes' shop window were a sight to behold. The Organ Society has continued its popularity with concerts by celebrity artistes since 1971, when enthusiasts restored the 'Christie' organ.

One tradition which has not survived the years is the ringing of the Pancake Bell. At eleven o'clock precisely, on Pancake Day, the church bell was rung to remind housewifes to make their pancakes. The ancient custom originated before clocks and watches were common usage. However, about 1924 the custom seems to have lapsed and 'Merry Shrovetide' with its feasting and merriment is past history.

Hawton ❧

Hawton is a small village, situated a mile east of the Fosse Way (A46). The river Devon flows into the Trent nearby. There is evidence of Saxon settlement, indeed the Saxon name 'Holtun' means a 'farm in the hollow'. The village is mentioned in the Domesday Book as having five manors and two churches. After the Conquest in 1066, the king dispossessed the landowners and gave the land to Robert de Linesi, from whom it passed through various families until in the 15th century it was sold to Sir Thomas Molyneux.

The 13th century church, built by Sir Robert de Compton, is famous for its Easter Sepulchre and the fine stone carvings, including the tomb of its founder. The east window is thought to be one of the finest of its type in England. The Perpendicular tower was added to the church in the 15th century by Sir Thomas Molyneux, and it is said that King Henry VII followed the progress of the battle of Stoke from its battlements.

During the Civil War, earthworks were built opposite the church and a larger fortification known as the Queen's Sconce was erected a short distance away for the protection of Newark.

The size of the village changed dramatically in 1933 when the boundaries changed. The area to the north was sold for housing development so that Hawton lost much agricultural land, its local pub Spring House, its mill and and its wharf. Some families no longer lived within the parish. A nine hole golf course was also sold for housing.

The village school, opened in 1859, was so reduced in numbers that it closed, with the few remaining children being transferred to Newark schools. A population of 377 in 1921 declined to less than 60 after the boundary changes.

Gypsum has been quarried at Hawton for nearly a century and is still the largest gypsum working in Britain. It was formerly Cafferatas but is now owned by British Gypsum. Some years ago there was a thriving brickmaking and coal business in the village, also a brass and iron foundry owned by William Bailey. The firm of Thomas Scales & Co had a cotton and bleach works at Hawton Mill, but these are now all gone. There is still no shop, post office or pub in Hawton, and the village is poorly served by public transport. The village hall was built by two unemployed village youths during the recession of the late 1920s, and is maintained by a hall committee.

The legend of St Catherine's Well is a romantic story of the village maiden and her two admirers. Isabel was in love with Sir Everard Bevercotes but his rival for her affections, Sir Guy Saucenier, slew Sir Everard in a jealous rage. Where he fell there gushed a fountain of pure water, whch still flows to this day. This sad event occurred on St Catherine's Eve and the water, reputed to have medicinal healing powers, still flows into St Catherine's Well, situated in nearby Devon Park.

Hickling

Known in Saxon times as Echeling, Hickling is situated on the western edge of the Vale of Belvoir. This is a small village, pleasantly mixing modern houses with traditional red brick cottages and farms, and visitors are soon aware that agriculture is still an important village activity.

To many people, Hickling is best known for the 'basin' of the Grantham Canal. Completed in 1797, the canal carried coal, building materials and agricultural products until about 1930. Thereafter, it fell into steady decline. Recently the Grantham Canal Preservation Society have cleared the Hickling basin, where the resident flock of ducks and swans attract many visitors.

Not far from the canal is St Luke's, a church of great charm standing well back among trees. With its wide nave, square headed clerestory window and long chancel, the church was largely rebuilt in the 19th century, although incorporating a number of older features. The windows incorporate many fragments of ancient glass, the door is 13th century and patterned with scrolls and leaves and a 600 year old gravestone is built into an outside wall.

Perhaps the most exciting relic is a 1,000 year old cover of a Saxon tomb, with its mass of fine carving.

Hickling was apparently the home of an anonymous engraver of headstones whose many products, in archaic style, are widespread across the Vale of Belvoir. One such stone, with an angel in shallow relief across the top, is that of John Smith who died at Hickling in 1725. The inscription reads:

> 'This world's a city full of crooked streets
> Death is the market place where all men meets
> If life were merchandise that men could buy
> The rich would often live and poor men dies.'

Holme Pierrepont

Holme Pierrepont was put on the map with the opening of the British National Water Sports Centre. Residents of the parish of Holme Pierrepont watched in fascination as out of the meadows and the quarries came the Olympic-sized rowing course. This was followed by the planting of trees and shrubs. Then grassy hillocks, fishing ponds and walks developed. This was especially pleasing to the local inhabitants as a few years earlier the Central Electricity Board had put forward plans for a power station here.

Over the last few years the Water Sports Centre has grown, the latest addition being the wild-water slalom, although it must be said it is not all water sports. In winter months the birds are an added attraction, many being water fowl and herons. In cold frosty weather, when the rowing course ices over, watching them perform on the slippery surface is as good as any Walt Disney nature film.

The village is situated just beyond the water skiing area. This is composed of a handful of houses, varied in size and type, many now taken over by people who work in Nottingham. In the parkland stands Holme Pierrepont Hall and the small but beautiful church of St Edmond. The first church was built in the 13th century and extended in the 17th. It holds the tombs of the Manvers family. The church now comes into the Radcliffe-on-Trent group of parishes and is looked after by a priest-in-charge. It has a small but loyal congregation which swells in numbers when Jimmy Saville (a friend of the vicar) comes for one weekend in November. It is a very busy weekend of social and sporting events. A considerable amount of money is raised and goes to local charities. Some of the most down-to-earth people have been known to get a glimpse of the ghost of the 'White Lady' on these occasions!

Hoveringham

Hoveringham is a village on the banks of the river Trent between Nottingham and Newark and quite a large village. There are many old buildings, with some inevitably being renovated, and made into very desirable residences.

When the baker's shop closed down some years ago, the village was left with one general shop-cum-post office, together with two public houses and a church. It is ostensibly a farming community with corn and sugar beet being grown and cows being kept. There are few residents left in the village who were born here.

The large Hoveringham Gravels concern grew from this small village and, while the business is still here, it became part of the giant Tarmac Group a few years ago.

Kelham

Kelham, or Kelum as it was spelled in the 12th century, has grown up around a crossing of the river Trent. Early bridges crossed the river upstream of the present one, somewhere near the church. Evidence of foundations of buildings have been found south of the church, which suggests that the settlement was originally in this area, and that possibly a major flood forced a move to the present site.

The village is an old farming community which grew up as part of the estate to serve the lords of the manor of Averham and Kelham, providing employment for most of the inhabitants. Some families have lived in the village for several generations. The farms have amalgamated since the 1950s, reducing employment opportunities. A large proportion of the residents are retired, with the younger people working in nearby Newark. Very little development has been allowed, with the result that the population is static at around 100. In the 1891 census there were 224 inhabitants.

Kelham played an important part in the farming industry, when the estate was used to develop the technique of growing sugar beet when it was introduced to this country during the First World War. The Kelham sugar beet processing factory was built in 1921. It is now known as the Newark factory and is one of the largest and most modern sugar factories in Europe.

The Hall was the manor house of the Sutton family, who were an illustrious family in the county going back to the Norman Conquest. They served their Crown and Country with distinction for generations: the most notable being Robert Sutton who was a very close supporter of Charles I. The King was given shelter in the village during the Civil War, while trying to make contact with his supporters under siege in Newark. Legend has it that he hid in a house in Blacksmith Lane immediately before his arrest. He took communion in the church; the silver chalice he used is now in the treasury of Newark parish church. Villagers sheltered from Cromwell's army in Kelham church and plugged holes can be seen in the north door, where they had placed weapons to protect themselves.

The mausoleum attached to the church was built by Bridget, Duchess of Rutland, in memory of her father, Robert Sutton, 'in gratitude to the most indulgent and best father'. Reclining statues of Robert and his wife Margaret lie atop the vault, with their ancestry and achievements recorded on the base. The present Hall was built in 1854, the third one on the site with the previous two having been destroyed by fire. In 1903, mortgagees sold off the Hall and extensive farmland.

Next occupants of the Hall were a group of monks, led by Father Herbert Kelly, who founded the Society of the Sacred Mission or SSM. They trained men for missionary work, and later for the Church of England ministry. They were known worldwide as 'The Kelham Fathers'.

Father Kelly was responsible for the planting of an extensive collection of trees in the hall grounds, some of which have grown into excellent specimens. The grounds are now one of three sites designated by the 'Men of Trees' for memorial planting by individuals. The SSM cemetery is just outside the church wall.

During the Second World War, the SSM were host to many military and civilian groups. The Texans were the most exciting with their oil drilling rigs, stetsons and unusual beer drinking habits. They demanded that the salt cellar was always on the bar at the 18th century Fox Inn, to make the local brew more to their taste. The first drilling for oil in the United Kingdom was in a field in Kelham in 1919 by Thomas D'Arcy. Small traces were found, but lack of money forced abandonment. D'Arcy went on to found a worldwide oil exploration company, returning to Kelham Hills in the 1940s, to find oil and a small field was established.

In 1973 the Newark and Sherwood District Council was formed. New headquarters were needed and the availability of the Hall made it an ideal choice.

Keyworth

Keyworth, once a very small village in the south of the county, now has a population of about 10,000, housed in large estates at each end of the old village.

The year 1880 was very significant for the small village of Keyworth, this was the year that Plumtree station was opened. Goods could now be brought into the village in hours instead of days. Farmer's drays would take anything up to two days to deliver coal from as far away as Gedling pit. The price being still only 12s 6d per ton when brought to Plumtree station by train was indeed a step forward.

The main industry was farming, there being twelve farms and four smallholdings. Sadly today only three remain.

Hosiery manufacturing employed many, including women. The women, not able to leave their homes to work at the workshop (of which there were ten known as stockingers' shops) did seaming at home by candlelight. This could not have been easy. 1959 saw the last of the hosiery trade in Keyworth, which has been replaced by various small factories.

Gone are the days when the village was served by small shops trading from a room in a dwelling house. There were five such shops, one bakehouse and the Co-operative shop which was owned by the villagers. Three supermarkets now provide all the provisions for the village and the surrounding areas.

The first school teacher was a disabled seamstress, the church belfry was used as a schoolroom until such time as the National school was built. Parents were charged one penny per week for each child. As this was a Church of England school, nonconformist parents refused to allow their children to attend. This state of affairs existed until the council school was built. This school no longer exists, having been demolished to make way for senior citizen's dwellings. Three junior schools and one comprehensive school now provide education for the children of Keyworth and the surrounding villages.

With a population of only 900 at the start of the 20th century, it is a source of some pride that at least 30 professional cricketers went out of the village to play cricket. One man, by the name of Will Attewell, played for England. The cricket pitch in those days was a piece of ground in a field, fenced off to keep the cattle out. Today the village boasts two large playing fields, with facilities for football, cricket, bowls, tennis and a swimming pool.

The village has had its scandals. Legend tells of a tenant farmer, farming Church Farm, who was visited by the rector who had occasion to make a complaint. The said rector was whipped very soundly with a horse whip and sent on his way. The whip is still in existence and is owned by descendants of the farmer. What has not been made clear is the reason for the whipping – one can only speculate!

Early in 1988 the Keyworth Parish Council exchanged a parcel of land, known as the 'Stone Pits', for a piece of land through which the Fairham Brook meanders. This is now known as the 'Keyworth Meadow' (conservation area). It consists of damp grassland, with willow and ash trees, and there are also four ponds. The area is an excellent one for birds, and various species of butterfly have been seen. Over 60 species of flora have been identified and the fox and the hare also visit the area.

Kilvington 🌿

This is a small hamlet of about ten houses but has its own dear little church, hidden from the road but approached by a narrow lane which runs adjacent to the main thoroughfare. A century ago the church was used as a sheep fold, but in 1892 it was brought back into use as a church and still has a medieval chalice and paten dug up in 1897.

As with other neighbouring villages the area has been extensively mined for gypsum, which has now ceased. The land is still awaiting restoration but in the meantime quite extensive varieties of bird life make use of the water-filled pits. There is a nice footpath which goes across the river Devon to Staunton, virtually joining both villages' churches.

Kinoulton 🌿

Situated on the fringe of the Vale of Belvoir, Kinoulton is little more than a mile from the Fosse Way. The descent into the village from the Fosse provides a lovely panorama encompassing not only the village, but the whole of the Vale across to Belvoir Castle, standing sentinel-like on the edge of the Wolds.

In the 12th century, the village boasted a castle, and it is believed that Archbishop Cranmer had a palace here; there are records of a village school going back over 700 years, and on a hill to the west of the village there is a spring which was famous as a spa in Georgian times, much valued for its 'considerable medicinal virtues.'

Today, however, Kinoulton is largely a commuter village, blending the traditional farms and cottages with modern houses in a ribbon nearly a mile long.

On the northern edge of the village, there is an area dominated by an avenue of poplars, a landmark which can be seen from all approaches. This is a bridleway leading up to Vimy Ridge Farm and Kinoulton Gorse. The trees were planted by Sir Jesse Hind, a wealthy Nottingham solicitor, whose son 'Monty' was killed at Vimy Ridge during the First World War. It is said that the trees, 188 in all, represent the officers who died in the action.

During the years of 'the Depression' Sir Jesse employed many ex-servicemen's sons and the large huts where they lived, though in ruins and overgrown, can still be seen at Vimy Ridge. The whole farm, once a scene of busy activity, is now empty and derelict, as though damaged in war.

The eastern end of Kinoulton is dominated by the village green and the Nevile Arms, proudly bearing the arms of the Earls of Gainsborough. Bought by Sir Jesse Hind in 1928, he changed the name to the Hind Arms, against the wishes of the locals who later successfuly petitioned for the name to revert to the original. On the green stands the splendid Turkey oak, perhaps commemorating victory in the Crimea.

Until the 18th century, the village was served by the church of St Wilfrid, high on the hill to the west of the village. However, by the end of that century the church was abandoned and in ruins, remote from the village which by then was at the foot of the hill more than half a mile away. Today, only the foundations of the old church can still be seen under the turf, but many graves remain, some with slate headstones in remarkable condition and as legible today as when new up to three centuries ago. However, perhaps not all have survived. Writing about Kinoulton, Roy Christian says that 'according to a local story, grave-stones were used by the village baker to line his oven, a misdemeanour that was exposed when a customer noticed that his loaf bore the imprint "in loving memory"!'

The present church is late Georgian, built of brick with classical proportions but somewhat restrained decoration. In the porch a plaque informs us that it was built by Henry, Earl of Gainsborough in 1793. With the old church on the hill in ruins, the Neviles, though Roman Catholic, considered it their duty to provide a new church. A carved stone from the old church was placed at the foot of the south wall to show continuity with the new.

Visible through the trees a short distance from the church is the old vicarage, perhaps the most impressive house in Kinoulton. Built in 1849 for the Rev Thomas Charlewood, it was an early major commission for T. C. Hine, later to become the most distinguished Nottingham architect of his time.

Kinoulton has the distinction of having been a Peculiar. This meant that the vicar had the power to hold a civil court, to punish any offences committed against his church; he also had the power to grant marriage licences and hold a probate court for proving wills. The origin of these privileges undoubtedly lies in the fact that the Archbishop of York possessed a residence in the village. However, the privileges were abolished by law in 1857.

Kirklington 🌿

Kirklington was called in medieval times Kyrtelington, but was entered in the Domesday Book as Cherlington.

The church is dedicated to St Swithin and is partly Norman. It consists of a nave, large chancel and a tower with four pinnacles containing three bells dated 1604, 1727 and 1759. The clock in the tower is in memory of the men of the parish who fell in the First World War.

Farming still goes on at Whip Ridding, Meadow Farm, Hall Farm and Home Farm. Very few families in the village derive their income from Kirklington today. Most commute to Nottingham, Mansfield, Southwell and London. There are 234 persons on the electoral roll.

There are many old customs associated with the village. Kirklington Feast was always held on the first Sunday in October. All sons and daughters working away from home, married or in service went home for Feast Sunday. Two stalls were set up in front of the Whetham Arms (now Ivy Farm House) on Saturday evening and did a good trade in sweets, oranges, brandy snaps and gingerbread.

Plough Monday was always kept on the second Monday in January when the farmworkers of the village went the rounds of the village and acted a play in every house where they were invited. They were given mince pies and ale or money. The exit lines of the play were:

> 'We are the country plough lads
> That go from door to door
> Good Master and Good Mistress
> As you sit by your fire
> Remember us good plough lads
> That work through mud and mire
> So bring us out a good pork pie
> And a jug of your best beer
> We wish you all good night
> And another Happy Year'

The parish roads were let every year from 1st May to the end of September. Two or three cottagers usually joined together to pay the charge of £6 and put three cows each on the road verge. This grazing kept the grass verges close and fine almost like a lawn. One day each year the villagers were allowed free run of the woods to pick blackberries. The village school closed for the day and whole families took picnics into the woods.

The treble bell was rung every Sunday morning at 8 am whether there was an early service or not. It was also rung at 11 am on Shrove Tuesday to warn housewives to begin cooking their pancakes.

To provide Christmas beef, a fat beast (estate fed) was slaughtered at the slaughterhouse near the hall stableyard and butchered. The villagers came with large baskets and to each was given according to the size of his family. It was distributed on the afternoon of the shortest day of the year after the rent had been paid in the morning. Rent was paid twice a year on the longest and the shortest day. Lunch was provided for all rent payers on those two days. The custom lapsed during the First World War.

There used to be a very good sheep wash by the roadside on the Northern Dyke. There is a large, stone half-moon-shaped trough in which a couple of men could stand and lean over the rounded side (which jutted into the stream) and wash the sheep. Sheep were brought from many parishes round about and the money taken, together with that from lane letting, put towards parish expenses. The sheep wash was closed in 1930. All local farming is now arable.

If you look at the pulpit in the church you will see that in the sides are some holes filled with more recent wood. The explanation is that a sporting rector, at the beginning of the 19th century, used to have the pulpit, which was loose from its base, carried down on weekdays to a swamp in the parish frequented by wild duck, when it served as a screen for the parson who fired on the birds through holes made for that purpose.

Lady Bay 🦢

Lady Bay is an area adjacent to West Bridgford. To the inhabitants it is known as 'the island', being bounded on one side by the river Trent and on the other by the Grantham Canal.

There are several theories as to the origin of the name Lady Bay. The earliest goes back to AD 910 when Aethelflaeda, the Lady of the Mercians, ordered a 'Burgh' or fortress to be built on the south side of the Trent. 'Lady Bay' may have been a corruption of 'The Lady's Burgh'.

Another possibility refers to a chapel which stood on Trent Bridge in the 13th century, dedicated to St Mary, which might have given the name 'Lady's Bay' to a bend in the river.

Yet again in 1815, a historian of Nottingham, advanced the theory that a plot of land, now known as the Hook, was the pasture of 'My Lady's Bay Mare' or simply a mare called 'Lady Bay'.

Another link with history can be found in the fact that a little Saxon church once stood on a site at Adbolton, not half a mile from Lady Bay, and bore the name All Hallows, the name adopted in 1942 by the parish church of Lady Bay.

There have been times when the inhabitants of Lady Bay would have wished the river and canal were further away from their homes. In 1947 the Trent, carrying extra water down from thawing snow in the Derbyshire hills, flooded the fields to an alarming depth on one side, and the canal rose on the other, so that it only required the flood level to rise a further couple of inches for the houses in Lady Bay to have been waterlogged.

Up to the late 1920s, Lady Bay was little more than half its present size, with the area near the canal being fields and rough ground, and it is interesting to walk through the roads between Trent Boulevard and the canal and see the demarcation line where the 'old' houses built in the late

1800s and early 1900s give way to the newer ones constructed in the later 1900s.

It is understood that at one time a large part of Lady Bay was orchard, and one can still see several small brick buildings which it is said were used by night watchmen guarding the fruit in the autumn before it was sent to market.

One large house on the corner of Holme Road and Julian Road was at one time owned by a Mr Watts, whose shop 'The Lustre Mantle Co.' at the bottom of Hound's Gate was well known for the sign which appeared every year at the end of June – 'The Longest Day Has Passed Away, Prepare For The Longest Night'. Mr Watts built a factory linked to the house by an overhead bridge. Every week a railway delivery cart drawn by a horse would rumble down Holme Road carrying rolls of raw paper, which when processed would appear again as 'Miss Muffet Toilet Rolls'.

In the 1950s Lady Bay's first public house was opened. Before this, the residents had to go up to Trent Bridge for their liquid refreshment, and there were stories of those who, not wishing to go so far, would surreptitiously go to the off licence on Trent Boulevard with all manner of bags, including violin cases, to conceal their purchases from prying neighbours.

Although now a suburban, rather than a rural area, this is nevertheless a compact community, catering for the young with clinics, playgroups and junior schools, right through to clubs for the senior citizens. The local shops provide most needs, whilst spiritual welfare is taken care of in the churches.

Lambley ❧

Lambley – the field where the lambs were reared. The village retains some of its grass fields, where grazing sheep and lambs give a picture of rural tranquillity and remoteness in spite of its closeness to Nottingham, which is only six miles away to the south.

This sense of isolation is, in part, due to the fact that the village lies along the bottom of a horseshoe-shaped valley formed by the branches of the Cocker Beck, which then flows east towards Lowdham and into the river Trent. The streams have eroded deep narrow gullies through the clay until they meet the hard skerry known as waterstone, then small weirs or waterfalls are formed. Over a long period of time the sides of the

The view to the west from Green Lane, Lambley

gullies have become covered with trees so that today they present pleasant wooded valleys up to 20 feet deep which in spring are carpeted with wild flowers. These valleys are referred to by their local name of the Dumbles and provide attractive walks and adventure playgrounds for children. Its sense of remoteness is also due to the lack of any major road, railway or navigable waterway passing through the village. The first bus service started in the late 1920s.

After Domesday, the manor of Lambley was held by the Cromwell family and it was here that Lord Ralph Cromwell was born in 1394. He was to achieve distinction as Lord Treasurer of England to Henry VI and was responsible for presenting the first budget to Parliament. Although Lord Ralph became a rich and powerful magnate, building Tattershall Castle, he must have retained his links with Lambley as he left instructions in his will that 'the church should be built and constructed anew'. The church is a fitting memorial to him, being one of the few almost entirely Perpendicular churches in Nottinghamshire. Outside on either side of the east window are two carved panels showing Cromwell's badge of a purse, representing his office as Lord Treasurer. After Cromwell's death the manor fell into disrepair and the site has remained an open space known as the Pingle. Traces of a moat can be seen in the field.

Lambley remained very much an agricultural community until the early 19th century when it expanded as a framework knitting village. By

102

1844 there were 381 stocking frames. The knitters worked the frames in their own homes in front of the long, small-paned windows which distinguish a framework knitter's cottage. It is unfortunate that many of the cottages have been modernised and the distinctive windows removed. It is possible to find a few on Main Street and Green Lane and to see where former windows have been bricked up or altered.

Until fairly recently the first Sunday in May was celebrated as Cowslip Sunday. People came from Nottingham and elsewhere in 'brakes' or on bicycles to buy cowslips at one old penny per bunch. Refreshment stalls were set up along Main Street and Church Street and it is said that extra policemen were drafted in to deal with the crowds. Sadly, very few cowslips grow wild now but they can still be found in a few secluded hedgerows. It is said that there was a special hymn only sung on Cowslip Sunday, but it appears to have been lost in time.

During the early part of this century a brass band was founded by Fred Booth, the licensee of the Woodlark Inn. Mr Potter of Lambley House bought instruments and uniforms and the band practised every Sunday in the old factory on Main Street. On one occasion the band was playing Christmas carols when it marched straight into a haystack!

Lamcote ⚜

Lamcote is an area between Radcliffe-on-Trent and Holme Pierrepont, which was originally a very rural area but by the 1920s most of the buildings housed tradesmen and businesses.

The most prominent building was Lamcote House, which was the home of Mr and Mrs Charles Birkin. It was a very large house with fine gardens and stables where racehorses were trained and was an occasional meeting place for the local hunt. Over the years the Duke of Windsor was known to be a frequent visitor to the house and local gossip was rife over the friends he brought with him! Lamcote House gradually went into decline, finally being turned into flats before eventually being de-molished. Private houses now occupy the site.

Lamcote Farm covered a large area with horses and cattle etc, but later most of the land was built on to house Canadian airmen and their families and is still known locally as the 'Canadian Estate', despite the houses being in private ownership for over 20 years.

The old Primitive chapel was made into a general grocer's where you could once buy a cup of mixed pickles for a penny. The Co-operative premises were a double fronted shop with a bake-house at the rear, next door to a butcher's shop, stables and slaughterhouse. Wheelwrights also had premises where you could stand and watch the whole waggon being made. They closed down in their third generation. Various malt rooms were in operation and the Red Lion public house eventually transferred its licence to the Trent Hotel, which is still in use today, the Red Lion now being a private residence.

A house resembling Anne Hathaway's cottage was known as the 'old Mud House' because of it being built of clay and wattle. A profusion of flowers always grew around this house making it very picturesque. Many businesses and shops have changed over the years and today the area is mainly private houses (with more still to be built) and Lamcote has been enveloped into Radcliffe village, although the name of Lamcote still lives on.

Langar 🦢

Langar is a small village standing on a small escarpment which slopes towards the Stroome and stretches from Langar to the west end of Barnstone. The Saxons are believed to have named this area 'The Lang Ridge', which is thought to be the origin of the name.

There is a fine church in the Early English style. The memorials of the Chaworth family, who once owned Wiverton Hall, are in the north transept. On the opposite side of the chancel are the memorials to the Scroope family. Admiral Lord Howe, a descendant of the Scroopes, led the English Navy to defeat the French in the 'Battle of the Glorious First of June'. He became known as 'Black Dick of Langar'. The victory is still celebrated each year by the present owner of Langar Hall.

There have been two previous houses of importance. The first was built by Lord Scroope in the 15th century and later converted to 18th century standards by the Howe family. The present house, a much smaller building, was built in the reign of William IV.

A year or so before the first Education Act, Mr Francis Wright, who lived at Langar Hall, saw the need for primary education in the village and built Langar its first school, which is still being used as the infants department. There is an annexe on the Barnstone Road. The rectory, a very attractive Queen Anne building, was the birthplace of the writer Samuel Butler. It became too impractical and expensive to be used as a home for the parish priest so it was sold and now rejoices in the name of Langar House. Langar is one of a number of parishes in the Wiverton group and the vicar now has a modern rectory at Cropwell Bishop.

The Unicorn's Head, another attractive building, is an early 18th century inn and provides a meeting place for people of the district. The village hall at Barnstone is used by both villages. Langar airfield is adjacent to the village where, during the Second World War, AVRO aero engines were repaired. Although now the larger part of the airfield is an industrial estate, a gliding school operates from there and many charitable parachute jumps take place.

In the past 20 years, two small private estates have been built which have blended into their surroundings and now look as if they have been there as long as some of the other properties.

Laxton ✑

Laxton is a small village set amid the Dukeries and mentioned in the Domesday Survey of 1086. The name is a derivation from Lexington, Lessington and Laxington. Its main claim to fame is the survival of the medieval open field system of farming. Books have been written and films, television and radio programmes made about Laxton.

At the beginning of the 20th century the school was in two parts, the 'Big' school, now used as Laxton village hall, and the 'Little' school on the opposite side of the street. The school day started with assembly and prayers. The infants recited their alphabet and reading began with three letter words and counting with the aid of a bead-frame. Children from the neighbouring village of Egmanton also attended, walking to and fro each day. The Laxton children ran home for dinner at mid-day, but not before saying a lengthy Grace and another prayer on their return.

There were, however, special treats throughout the year including a Christmas party in the parish room with a real tree. People who were very poor were served soup and bread from the vicarage. In October Laxton was transformed with lights, music and showmen in caravans behind the Dovecote Inn, celebrating the Feast of St Michael the Archangel, after whom the church is named. Nowadays Harvest Thanksgiving is held as near as possible to Laxton Feast Day. The harvest itself was collected with the help of horses and corn cut with scythes. Today, of course, tractors and combine harvesters are used. The corn was once ground in the mill which stood in Mill Field until 1916, where now the spot is marked by a ring of trees.

Children used to have organised trips to Thoresby Hall, where the lord of the manor lived. Tenants also had an annual dinner, a tradition still carried on, despite changes of landlord. On the first Monday in January, Plough Monday, ancient Mummer plays were enacted, a tradition which has sadly disappeared. Another important event was the Choir Supper, for the church had a very large choir.

Occupations in Laxton have changed, for once there was a full-time mole-catcher, a pig killer, two cobblers, a blacksmith, joiner and wheelwright. Many farmers brewed their own beer and one villager remembers she was often sent for 'a penn'orth of barm' for use in making bread.

Many students and visitors come to study Laxton's history, calling at the Visitor's centre which was opened in the grounds of the Dovecote Inn on 5th July 1986. They go to look at the castle grounds, where only traces of a castle now remain. They study a map of the open fields standing within the pound, once used for stray cattle. The Jury and the Court Leet and strip farming carry on despite the advancement in farming methods.

The Levertons

South Leverton is an attractive village, much larger in area than North Leverton, but with a population of only 450. It has seen few new buildings and so has retained the majority of its agricultural land. Its church, All Saints, built on a hill and half hidden from the south and east by tall trees, survives as one of the oldest and most picturesque in the district. Written evidence says that a Saxon church stood on the present site, but little of this remains apart from some 'long and short' walling in the vestry. Other remains belong to the Norman church which stood here about 1120 to 1180.

Opposite the church is the old Sampson's free grammar school. In 1688 the benefactor John Sampson gave this wonderful old school, in the days when education was just being organised in this county. Later in the 1900s it became the Church of England school under the jurisdiction of Notts County Council. It was a sad time for the village when it closed in July 1968 and like many other village schools was sold for a private dwelling. A few yards down the road is the old chapel, built in 1847, where the walls once rang with well-known Methodist hymns.

106

The first house in Meeting House Lane is Quaker Cottage, so-called because in 1650 it was given to the Quakers for their meeting place. The yard surrounding the house had several headstones in memory of those who had died in the belief of the Creed. Today it is a magnificent property in beautiful surroundings.

Another notable building in the village is the Priory. Built in 1166 of water quarry stone quarried in the parish, with quoins of dressed stone and walls four feet thick, it is historically connected with the church and is today a nursing home, the staff of which come mainly from the two villages.

Previously the social life of the village was enjoyed in the old Vicar's Room which stands behind the Plough Inn, an 'olde worlde' pub. The present Memorial Institute was built to commemorate the fallen in the First World War and many functions for both villages are held there. Today the village supports only the post office/general store and over the past few years two garden nurseries have been established.

Going from South to North Leverton you pass along an avenue of lime trees. There is parkland on your left in which stands a lovely old house, the original owner of which planted the trees in the early 1800s. Opposite is the famous cricket field where cricket has been played since the early 1900s. Players and spectators had their refreshment at the Railway Inn, just south of the railway crossing, from which the parish magazine takes its name.

Just over the crossing into North Leverton the sign says 'North Leverton with Habblesthorpe'. This was described in an earlier edition of the Guinness Book of Records as the longest multiple place name in England. Originally the two names referred to separate communities but they united on 25th March 1884.

A large housing estate, built in 1967 for employees at the power stations, now stands on the site where the Leverton Feast was held annually. This was an ancient custom and welcomed newcomers to the village, when everyone gathered on the last weekend in September.

The 12th century church of St Martin, with its handsome doorway, is approached by crossing a bridge over a stream. The old headstones at the front have been removed and replaced with lawns and a remembrance area. A few yards from the village crossroads stands the Methodist chapel and across the road is a small Wesleyan Sunday school, built in 1838. In Habblesthorpe, anciently called Applesthorpe, the church of St Peter has long since ceased to exist. The old churchyard still remains however, although it is no longer used for interments. The 12th century manor house still stands.

Power stations dominate the area and since the 1960s three large housing estates and two smaller ones have been built on agricultural land, swelling the population to over 1,200. Gone is the term 'agricultural labourer' – now it is 'power station employee'.

Until recently there were three shops in North Leverton but now only the post office/general store exists. The Royal Oak Inn has been considerably refurbished and is now renowned for its good food, attracting visitors from far and wide. Since 1907 the village has had its own doctor's surgery and dispensary. This surgery not only covers North and South Leverton but also 22 other surrounding villages, a very large practice for one doctor. The old blacksmith's shop, which was revived in 1971 for about two years, has now been demolished to make way for the village playing field and tennis court.

The outstanding feature in the village is the windmill (formerly known as the Subscription Mill) which was built in 1813. It still plays an important role in local community life and is open to the public. It is the last working windmill in Nottinghamshire and one of the very few remaining in the country.

Linby

Linby is one of the prettiest villages in Nottinghamshire, even though until 1988 it had a working colliery in its midst.

It has a medieval church dedicated to St Michael and in the churchyard are the unmarked graves of 163 pauper children who were brought from London, during the time of the Industrial Revolution, to work in the thriving textile mills along the river Leen. They are said to have died victims of the harsh conditions in the mills, although it is thought that smallpox also took its toll.

The village has a stream running the length of the main street to join the Leen and at the narrowest point the stream is fenced to prevent cows getting in, although these days more modern traffic is always knocking it down.

The main features of Linby village are its two stone crosses and a maypole. The top cross has a rare seven-sided base, probably the only one in the country, and is known to have been renovated in 1869 after being damaged by the Puritans in the 1650s. The bottom cross was erected around 1660 to celebrate the Restoration of the Monarchy and has the stream running under its base. This cross is said to mark the former boundary of Sherwood Forest.

A row of cottages along the main street which were built in the 18th century to house the framework knitters have been tastefully renovated in recent years. The area was the scene of some very serious Luddite riots in 1812 when followers of 'Ned Ludd' were responsible for smashing 19 of the stocking frame machines.

The village has a modern primary school, opened in 1968 and built just behind the old Victorian Church school which was then taken over by the Nottinghamshire Girl Guide Association, renamed Hanson House and used as a residential centre for the county's Guides and Brownies.

Further along Main Street, next to the Horse & Groom, is Brook Farm. A former smallholding, the Notts County Council here runs a remarkably successful horticultural training unit for mentally and physically handicapped adults of all ages. This was somewhat of a pioneering project but is now copied all around the country. The unit grows vegetables, flowers, plants and fruit and keeps hens and ducks. A farm shop helps to offset expenses. The students travel daily by public bus services and the villagers wholeheartedly support the project. There is always a waiting list.

Limestone is quarried at Linby and in years gone by was used to build churches along the Leen valley but is now mostly used for gardens and rockeries.

Lowdham

Lowdham, eight miles from Nottingham, originally a settlement by a beck on the edge of Sherwood Forest, is now a large village divided by two main roads, the main Nottingham to Southwell road and the dual carriageway, constructed just prior to the Second World War. The parish church remains at the original site with all the shops and community buildings on the other side of the dual carriageway – so giving rise to the name, 'the village that ran away from the church'.

The parish church of St Mary the Virgin, probably founded in 1170, with a Norman font and tower, houses a stone effigy of a knight, Sir Jon de Ludham, whose son accompanied Edward III to the battle of Crecy. The village school has adopted this family's armorial bearings as its badge. Near the church is the Old Hall, Elizabethan in parts, formerly called Broughton Hall and which contains in its grounds a mound on which stood a defensive fortification in earlier days.

Lowdham was surrounded by at least ten corn mills. Only two actually stand in Lowdham itself and are now private houses, but the original mill wheels can still be seen.

One of Lowdham's most imposing residences, only recently demolished, was Lowdham Grange, occupied by Charles Storer MD, doctor, landowner and JP. This site, including two farms, was acquired by the Crown in 1930 and became the first 'open' Borstal. Young lads were marched to Lowdham from an institution in Middlesex and camped out while constructing the present buildings, known as Her Majesty's Young Offender Institution.

Another interesting building which can be seen from the main A6097 is 'The Hutt', which incorporates two railway carriages in the upper storey.

John Henry Browne, vicar of Lowdham in the Victorian era, was an influential character and was instrumental in restoring the then neglected church and raising money and grants to build the village school. The Victorian school building was in use up until 1988 but a new school has now been built and the old school will be converted into residential units, so changing the village street scene. The clock which projects from this building was provided by public subscription to commemorate the coronation of George V.

In the past all trades were represented in Lowdham and although this is not so today, Lowdham still boasts 17 shops and no less than five pubs. Work was mainly agricultural and horticultural, with framework knitting in the 19th century. Nowadays, Lowdham's working population mainly commutes to Nottingham. A percentage work at the Young Offender Institution or the Police Training Centre at the neighbouring village of Epperstone. Horticulture certainly played a large part in the life of the village in the past; Pearsons the seed merchants sold their products over a wide area and employed many. Some of their orchards still remain and this local interest is reflected in a flourishing Horticultural Society formed in 1893, who stage a Horticulture Show every August Bank Holiday.

In common with other villages, Lowdham had its own annual Feast Day. This is a very ancient festival held on the Patronal Festival of the parish church. Lowdham's was, and still is, held at the beginning of September on one of the festivals of St Mary the Virgin. This was a great time in the village, marking the end of the harvest. Many home-made pork pies were baked and there is a rumour that the Christmas puddings were made then and the first one eaten on Feast Sunday. This annual

Feast is still celebrated by a visiting fair which arrives during the first week in September.

In spite of the addition of many more houses over recent years, there still exist beautiful walks over the many footpaths bordered by wild flowers, over areas with picturesque names such as 'World's End', 'Mount Pleasant' and Red Lane, so called it has been suggested, from the blood which flowed from the battles fought on nearby fields.

Meden Vale 🦋

Meden Vale has a population of around 3,000 and was formerly called Welbeck Colliery Village until the name was changed in 1975.

The old village is mainly built on a hill and in the valley runs the river Meden, from which the new name was derived. The newer part of the village was built on adjoining grassland, to house the miners and their families who moved down from the North of England and Scotland when there was plenty of work in the local collieries. In recent years a complex called Melville Court was built, comprising mainly flats and bungalows for the elderly and infirm. Included in the complex is a community centre where they can meet and take part in various activities.

Welbeck Colliery was sunk on a site towards Gleadthorpe in 1913, and the village was built around the pit between 1925–27. The colliery surrounds are very attractive as the spoil heaps have been landscaped where possible and many trees and bulbs have been planted. There are now cows grazing on the heaps that have been grassed, a sight that was never expected a few years ago.

Gleadthorpe Government Experimental Farm is also part of this village, which employs about 45 people. It was taken over by the Ministry of Agriculture and Fisheries in 1949 and it is the only Ministry farm in the country which has a poultry unit. In an aerial photograph of Gleadthorpe there are signs of a Roman camp. A Greek coin was found by a schoolboy on Wood Hill some years ago.

In 1928 a Methodist church was built and is still very active although the Anglican church was demolished. There are now eight shops of various types, an infants and a junior school, a thriving Miners Welfare and the Three Lions public house. The village hall is used continually by various organisations.

Misterton ✺

Misterton has a population of approximately 2,000 and extends up to the Iron Bridge at West Stockwith, where the river Idle flows into the river Trent.

The village owes part of its prosperity to King Charles I, who appointed Sir Cornelius Vermuyden, a Dutch engineer, with a Dutch workforce, to drain the marshes known today as the Isle of Axholme. The reclaimed land proved to be excellent arable land which brought work to the area and so the village flourished.

Ancient farms dating back to 1600 intermingle with Victorian and Georgian architecture. Many public buildings built in the Victorian era are still in regular use, such as the Victoria Institute, Temperance Hall and Methodist church. There is a Victorian letter box set in the wall of a house in Station Street, reputed to have been in use since the introduction of the Penny Post.

In 1777 the Chesterfield Canal was opened, linking Misterton with other market towns. The clay cut from the canal was found to be ideal for brickmaking. Thousands of bricks were needed to build the canal locks and bridges. Several brickyards were set up by some of the men who had learned their skills from the canal kilns, and so the industry continued for many years.

Festivals known as Love Feasts were popular in the mid-1800s, which consisted of seed bread handed round in baskets and water served in two handled mugs. These mugs can still be seen in the Methodist church. The Misterton annual Feast drew large crowds in September, when Rootes brought their fairground which took up two fields near the church.

All Saints church was completely restored in the 1800s when the north aisle and tower were rebuilt, with the addition of the broach spire. The earliest rector recorded was in the year 1200.

Mr John Rookes founded the water mill in 1840, the water from the Chesterfield Canal being used to provide the power to grind the corn into flour.

Today Misterton is a busy village combining agriculture with heavy and light industry. There are now 16 shops, but it is said that at one time there were 30. The new Fire Station is very modern with the latest fire fighting equipment and is always quick on the scene in an emergency. A story of the Misterton Fire Service from 1940–1984 has been placed in a time capsule in the foundations of the new Fire Station for future generations.

There are many outside pursuits such as boating on the canal, Idle or Trent, also fishing, horse riding, walking and numerous other sports facilities on the sports field – or perhaps a friendly drink at the Red Hart by the church or the Packet by the canal would be enjoyable!

Morton 🎐

A small village, not much more than a hamlet, tucked away in the countryside some two miles from Southwell. A village you don't pass through – rather turn off to. So close is it to its neighbours, it is sometimes referred to as Morton cum Fiskerton (or vice-versa) or Morton near Bleasby. But you will find that the villagers themselves always refer to their village as just Morton – and proudly so.

Morton itself is a scattering of houses and farms separated by fields and agricultural land and has remained this way mainly due to the firm belief in conservation by the villagers, and by local Parish and District Councils. Despite the growth in trade from the river traffic in neighbouring Fiskerton, Morton historically has been more involved with farming, its population showing little change from 1801–1901 at 101, with mild fluctuations in between.

There is much history attached to Morton. The small red brick church of St Dennis built in 1756 seats barely 70. Yet gravestones in the churchyard date from well before then and the first date on the register is 1680. All of which leads one to believe the existing church was built on the remains of a much older one.

The old school, just across the road from the church, dates from 1849. Before then however, the 'Daybill charity' was established by the will (in 1695) of a Richard Daybill of Morton, of 50 shillings a year for the education of poor children in Morton and Fiskerton. The money was obtained by tithes on land in Fiskerton called Little Close, Great Close and Spowage Close, all then adjoining fields separated by hedges. The money was of course paid to the school from 1849 but even though there is now no school in Morton, the 50 shillings is still paid by the present owner of the land to the Parish Council of Morton.

The friendly village pub has kept the name The Full Moon since

1844, when it was believed to have been built. It is a popular gathering place for the locals, so much so that many prefer to keep quiet about their excellent hostelry! But it is always that much busier on race meeting days at Southwell racecourse, which is barely two miles from Morton. Just down the road from The Full Moon is the old pinfold, or pound, recently restored using old stone from the area.

Morton is a village of sleepy beauty and charm; where agricultural and livestock farmers, business people and retired villagers live and work together. There is a lot of activity on the social side whether at cricket, football or on the tennis courts, social gatherings in the Old School House or the village pub. It is also a village where building has been carefully controlled and where the new blends well with the old.

Normanton on Soar

Normanton on Soar lies in a valley, bounded by the river Soar in the west and hills in the east. Its name is derived from the Anglo-Saxon 'Northman's Tun' meaning Northman's Farm. The name was first used between AD 870 and 940.

The focal point of the village is St James' church on the river bank, built in the early 13th century with a tall broached spire, considered the best example in the country. It suffered a disastrous fire in 1986 but is now restored.

The sites of two chapels in the village, Wesleyan and Baptist, have been taken over for housing.

Near the church is a hand-operated chain ferryboat, in use since 1901, to ferry the public across the river Soar to join up with Leicestershire footpaths. Nearby is a thatched timber-framed cottage of cruck construction dating from 1454, which is a popular subject for painters.

The village boasts a 17th century manor house with Dutch gabled dovecote, where garden parties were held which rivalled those of Buckingham Palace when Sir John Burn-Murdoch was in residence. Each time a boy was born in the village he was heard to say 'another soldier'. The estate has long since been split up for houses.

There was a railway station until the Beeching axe fell in the early 1960s, and a maggot factory which used to fill the houses with flies when the windows were opened and permeate the village with a nauseating smell.

There used to be many farms but now few are left and villagers travel mainly to Loughborough for work.

The Plough Inn started life in the 16th century as a coal wharf and farm, the coal being transported by barge. One room was used as a mortuary in about 1930 when many Sheffield fishermen visited, got drunk and slept on the riverbanks. A few did not survive this supposedly convivial occasion.

North & South Wheatley

South Wheatley has a ruined church, St Helen's, with a churchyard still used for burials and an old manor house. The present owners of the manor house have converted the barns into an antiques business.

Since the 1960s a number of new dwellings have been built and street lighting added. Not many of today's inhabitants were born in the village. Many either work at the nearby power stations or in Sheffield, Retford or Gainsborough, some are self employed. North and South Wheatley are linked by a playing field and a new school, which at the present time has about 45 pupils.

North Wheatley has a Methodist chapel and the church of St Peter and St Paul, which has a tower and a fine peal of bells. Several features of the church were brought from the South Wheatley church and the dismantled church of West Burton, the site of the latter now forming part of the West Burton power station. However, the rarest possession of the church is the oak staircase inside the tower leading to the platform of the bellringers. Today the Methodists and Anglicans have a combined Sunday school and join together for worship in each other's buildings every month.

There is a curious brick house with the date 1673 and the arms of the Cartwright's in stone over the brick porch, known as 'the Old Hall', which is often painted by local artists. The brick columns and vase-like decorations, also of brick, are worthy of notice and the house has a certain dignity.

There used to be two public houses in the village but only one, the Sun Inn, now remains. Other amenities include a village shop cum post office, an ice cream maker, mobile greengrocer and a freezer shop on the nearby bypass. The village hall stands on the playing field, which is home to a thriving cricket club, football, tennis and bowling clubs.

The Old Hall, North Wheatley

In years gone by the village also had a windmill; this has now gone but a few small cottages remain. The old street names still endure, such as Low Pasture Lane, Top Street, Low Street, Stone Lane etc.

The village is surrounded by farmland which is mainly used for sheep rearing and crop production but strawberries have also proved to be a popular crop and Wheatley strawberries have earned fame for delicious taste and quality and are supplied to a well known chain store and preserve manufacturers.

Transport has of course changed. One or two of the older villagers still remember being carried on wagons and drays, especially when there was a Primitive Methodist church in the village and on the annual Sunday school outing everyone went round the village on drays singing and then picnicked in a barn on Low Street.

North and South Wheatley have a combined Parish Council with three councillors from the South and ten from the North and they meet at approximately monthly intervals.

North Clifton 🖋

North Clifton at one time could boast a blacksmith, two tailors, two millers, a shoemaker, a shopkeeper, a carrier and a joiner. Now it is purely residential, despite existing in the shadow of one of the Trent valley power stations.

The river Trent was once crossed by a ferry in the next village of South Clifton and the inhabitants of North Clifton travelled free, provided they paid the ferryman a 'prime loaf' on Christmas Day, when he and his dog had, by custom, a good dinner at the vicarage.

Within the parish boundaries of North Clifton are the church of St George and the 'new' village school, but even these cannot really be claimed by the village as they are built in splendid isolation half way between North and South Clifton and jointly used by both parishes.

The school was built in 1876 for 70 children, with an addition in 1887, and although numbers have dropped it is still a thriving asset to the village.

The church is a lovely building, started in the 13th century, probably on the site of a pre-Conquest church. It has been added to over the centuries and has records starting in 1539. The interior has not been spoilt with plaster, leaving the original stonework showing. The windows date from the 15th century. At one time North Clifton had a collegiate chantry for secular priests, founded in the time of Edward II by Sir Richard Clifton. Now its chief claim to fame is a seat in the choir of Lincoln Cathedral.

In the village itself, apart from the post office, little evidence remains of its former self-contained existence. The old butcher's shop in Silver Street is now a workshop, although the wooden shutter is still over the window. The penny school is now a garage, but the bell which hangs in its original outside belfry still has pride of place.

Where the malt kilns stood, is now a garden of meditation, part of the Pure Lands Meditation Centre, for the learning and practising of relaxation and meditation, founded in 1972.

The Cross Keys public house is now a private house and so is the old Methodist chapel, built in 1858.

Even the hall, built in 1865 by Miss Freeth, has changed its role and is now a nursing home. However, above the stable block, the clock still sends out its 'Westminster' chimes every quarter of an hour. It still has annual services by the same Derby firm of John Smith, who installed it for the Miss Freeths in 1877.

Oldcotes

Oldcotes lies in the very north of the county around the junction of the A60 and the A634, just a little over one mile from the South Yorkshire border. In the Domesday Book it is recorded as being mostly wasteland with only six acres of meadowland – 'sufficient for four ploughs' plus two mills. The name of Ulecotes was given to the area in 1194 when one Gerard De Stirap, who lived in nearby Tickhill Castle, gave his eldest child Philip a piece of land for his own use. Ulecotes was his choice of name for his newly acquired piece of land.

Between Oldcotes and Blyth is one of only five licensed tournament fields in the country. King Richard granted this licence in 1194 when he tried to ensure that more and more of his subjects would be trained to take up arms against his enemies.

In the middle of the 19th century, whilst excavating prior to building St Helen's Catholic church, many tiles and animal bones were discovered and further excavation revealed the remains of a Roman villa. The floor turned out to be mosaic and it was thought to have been built around the time of Hadrian's Wall.

Also in the mid 1800s, when most of the land and the village belonged to Viscount Galway, the lines of the Manchester, Sheffield and Lincolnshire Railway Company were laid, which meant that the produce of the few farmers who owned their own land could be transported to a much wider area than previously. Other men and boys found themselves walking to employment at Shireoaks pit, the shaft of which was sunk in 1854. By 1861 Oldcotes was on a direct railway route to London and the North.

The half brick and half timber church is dedicated to St Mark. It was built in 1900 but in the late 1970s it was allowed to fall into disrepair as the congregation had dwindled to virtually nil. However, when in 1983 it was due to be sold or demolished, the village rallied round and would not allow this to happen. After consultations with the Archdeacon of Newark, a committee was formed and the church was renovated. And at the Harvest Festival in September 1983 the little church was once more full.

Mr William Moxon started his taxi service in 1949, which has developed into a thriving coach business. There is a garden centre and landscaping service as well as specialist water garden suppliers in the village.

Ollerton 🌿

Ollerton derives its name from the alder trees which are still grown along the banks of the river Maun, and was originally Alreton or Allerton meaning the 'farm among the alders'. Ollerton is recorded in the Domesday Book, when there were two manors owned by the Saxons Alwold and Wade.

The development of the village has been influenced by its position on the old road north from London to York, though the exact route changed over the years as it was little more than a sandy track through Sherwood Forest. The later road to York passed right through the village and was only bypassed in 1925. Ollerton was also on the road from Newark to Worksop and on the road from Mansfield to Lincoln. Consequently the village became a meeting place for Forest officials and local government officials and eventually the Hop Pole and White Hart became important inns as the London–Glasgow coach through Newark changed horses in the village.

The toll gates ceased to function on the Worksop to Kelham turnpike on 30th April 1878 and this caused such jubilation amongst the villagers who had faced such heavy expenses paying tolls that a celebration was held at the White Hart, attended by 400 people.

There were hop yards on the alluvial deposits of the river Maun and Rainworth Water, and there was a weekly hop market on Fridays. There was also a cattle market on May Day and another fair on 26th September. The village has now revived the ancient market rights by holding a Victorian street market just before Christmas. There are plans for another market in the summer months.

In 1853 when the population was at its highest there were over 20 shops in the village. There were two bakers, two blacksmiths, nine boot and shoe makers, three bricklayers, three butchers, one chemist, one draper, 13 farmers, three grocers, three joiners (two were also cabinet-makers), two maltsters, three milliners and dressmakers, two plumbers and glaziers, two saddlers, six tailors and two wheelwrights. There was a surgeon, a watchmaker and a hairdresser. Often people had more than one job or trade like Joseph Lister who kept the Hop Pole Inn and was also hop grower, farmer, maltster and postmaster. The largest occupation for many years until this century was hop growing.

Ollerton was owned by the Nevilles and later by the Markhams. The Markham family owned land in the area as early as 1260 but through marriage gained control of the manor during the reign of Elizabeth I. The family were staunch Catholics which led to persecution during the 16th century of both the family, their servants and villages influenced by the family. The Roman Catholic chapel was in the roof of the present building.

The Savile family, who had already owned Rufford Abbey since the early 17th century, bought all the Markham property for £22,000 in 1746. Ollerton Hall has not been occupied as a family seat since 1743 and has now been sold to become a Sue Ryder Home.

Several very old buildings remain in use including the post office, one of the oldest in Nottinghamshire, and the watermill. Watermills are recorded in use for many centuries for grinding corn. The present mill owned by the Mettam family is probably on the site of the Domesday Book mill. The mill grinds flour and animal feedstuff and flour for bread and cake making can be purchased.

Ollerton National school was founded in 1842 between Ollerton and Wellow and closed in the 1920s when schools opened in the colliery villages. The children were supposed to attend regularly but were often away to help in the fields with potato picking, stone picking, bird scaring or harvesting.

The church of St Giles stands on the site of an older chapel which was pulled down around 1777 due to its state of disrepair. The vicar now presides over the churches in Boughton and New Ollerton as well. There was also a Wesleyan chapel on Forest Road, now rebuilt, and a Primitive Methodist chapel on Station Road, now a private dwelling.

Orston ✑

Orston is a typical Vale of Belvoir village, with church, hall, school, farms, shop, pub and chapel. It is a thriving village community, still basically rural in character, but with many varied facets of life. Orston has around 100 houses, home to some 400 people.

The manor house was at the north end of High Street. Nothing remains of it today, except a find of treasure trove, 1,500 coins which had been buried in the grounds, probably during the Civil War.

Orston also has an interesting industrial history. Its gypsum workings go back to medieval times and were described as 'the finest in the Kingdom'. Today, all that remains of 'The Royal Plaster Works' in the centre of the village is a partially filled-in pit and outbuildings and some overgrown ponds on the outskirts of the village, which were once the most efficient plaster works in Europe. It nevertheless went bankrupt in 1873!

The site of what was a mill just outside the village is equally interesting. Records show a mill there since 1216. The last mill was dismantled in 1916, to be shipped to New Zealand to become its first working windmill.

There has been a significant change during this century in terms of the occupations of the inhabitants of Orston. Just before the Second World War, it was still primarily a farming community, with kindred trades still in evidence, including a miller, blacksmith, wheelwright, joiner and saddler. Today, there are fewer farms, with only two remaining herds of cattle and a few sheep. The old trades have gone, and most inhabitants now look outside Orston for their work. It is, however, far from a dormitory village, but retains an active community spirit in spite of a divergence of daytime pursuits.

There is still a variety of industry represented within the village, in addition to the residual farms – Orston is home to a mushroom farm, a haulage contractor, a feed supplier, a picture mouldings supplier and building and development firms. The fishmonger, Matty Gladders, has been supplying fish to the people of Orston for around 40 years.

The street names are interesting, with some of the original meanings now lost in history. Mill Lane, High Street, Smite Lane and Spa Lane are more obvious, though the mill has long since gone, High Street is no longer the main street, and the spa was never successfully commercially developed, although the chalybeate spring was said to be 'good for hypochondriacs'! It is more difficult to guess the basis of the names of Lordship, Loughbon, Launder and the City, and visitors to the village are often confused, particularly the car treasure hunt participants who are regularly seen in the summer months.

The parish church of St Mary is an attractive old building, with some medieval features, including wall paintings. It has recently been subject to restoration and decoration. The church houses a drum brought home from the Battle of Waterloo and it also has a fine set of bells, frequently rung by visiting teams of bell-ringers. The chapel is also a flourishing community, and there are many joint ventures between the Methodists and the Anglicans, including an annual Flower Festival.

Two traditional annual occasions, the Orston Feast and the Horticultural Society Exhibition, are sadly no more. There is, however, a 'new' tradition of which Orston is very proud – the Christmas Pageant, started by Toc H in 1965. It features the Angel Gabriel appearing to Mary from the roof of the village hall, Roman soldiers with flaming torches, Mary proceeding on a donkey down the village street to the 'stable' near the pub, the three Kings on horseback, shepherds, angels, all culminating with everyone squeezing into the church to sing carols. It is a most impressive and moving ceremony, attended by several hundred people, including many visitors from outside the village.

The population is well served with local facilities, including a post office and shop, visits from a mobile butcher, greengrocer, hairdresser and library. The village no longer has its own district nurse or policeman resident in the village, but at least it still has its own village postman!

The two riding schools have now closed down, but there is no shortage of horses and ponies in the village. Orston is on the boundary of two Hunts, and an annual meet takes place at the Hall, a most colourful occasion.

The river Smite runs close to the village, and this provides much entertainment for local children with their jamjars and sticks – more serious fishermen visit the nearby 'gravel pits', relics of the gypsum mining.

The village has only recently received the benefit of full street lighting and mains drainage – until the provision of the latter, a perhaps less delightful feature of Orston was the 'stinkdyke' – a facility which the local population was not too disappointed to lose!

Owthorpe

Nestling at the foot of the Wolds, Owthorpe lies just over a mile from the Fosse Way on the very edge of the Vale of Belvoir, not far from the Leicestershire border.

It is a small hamlet, mainly made up of 13 households, two of which are farms, with a few more cottages and farms scattered up to a mile away. All in all it is very much a rural community, and it is hard to believe that it is a mere ten miles away from the bustling centre of the city of Nottingham.

It is by no means a dormitory village, but has very much retained its country way of life, and in many ways could be classed as an isolated community. There are no street lights – save for the light which shines in the telephone box; there are no deliveries of national newspapers and the milkman only calls three times a week.

Despite its size, Owthorpe has its own small church (although services are only held fortnightly, and the vicar is shared with a nearby larger village), and a perhaps overlarge village hall. This has a capacity for 102 people while the main village population is just 22!

Owthorpe has always been a farming community, although the church and the small lake testify to the fact that there was once a manor house. This was the home of John Hutchinson, Governor of Nottingham Castle during the Civil War.

Anyone entering the cul-de-sac leading into Owthorpe village will first have to negotiate the many ducks and geese that frequently wander up and down the lane, and the sheep dogs that often try to herd them. Other obstacles that can block your progress are sheep, cows, pigs, chickens and a donkey. Owthorpe also happens to form a dividing line between the countryside used by two local hunts; the Quorn Hunt, and the South Notts Hunt. Both these Hunts attract many followers who more than outnumber the village population!

The community spirit which exists in Owthorpe is very strong, and all the annual events are well supported by most of the inhabitants.

Only two people work away from the village, and of the others, one half works on the land, and the others are self-employed. Their occupations include a builder, a tiler and a turf layer.

Oxton

Oxton has Saxon origins and is recorded in the Domesday Survey. It lies on the fringe of the old Sherwood Forest between Nottingham and Southwell. An ancient earthwork, Oldox Camp, covering about four and a half acres, looks upon the village from the north. The site may have been the original village of Oxton.

For over 400 years, the Sherbrookes have been lords of the manor and so Oxton was, and still is, an 'estate' village. Many of the inhabitants were tenant farmers or were employed on the estate. Some estate houses and cottages have been sold over recent years and their new inhabitants travel to Nottingham and surrounding areas for their livelihood.

In 1877 the Shipside family arrived. Both father and son were blacksmiths and, after taking over when his father retired, Tom Jnr entered into a contract with Raleigh Cycles of Nottingham to sell 50 cycles a year. Later, he set up a business selling cycles and motor cycles in premises at Daybrook. In 1911 he met William Morris (later Lord Nuffield), and entered into a contract to sell twelve Morris cars a year. This was the beginning of the firm of T. Shipside Ltd, selling Morris cars from extensive premises in Lower Parliament Street, Nottingham. It remained a family firm until 1961. The family were staunch Methodists and the village was to benefit in many ways from their generosity.

The village has had three chapels. The first, the Wesleyan Methodist chapel was built in the late 18th century. It still stands in Chapel Lane and is now a farm cottage. Its replacement was built in 1839 and it, also, has been made into a private dwelling. The Primitive Methodist chapel no longer stands. It was built near the Bridge Inn, in a field in which stood the cattle shed where the first services were held.

In the farmyard off Blind Lane can be found the tomb of Robert Sherbrooke, who died in 1710. His burial in this spot is possibly because it was the resting place of the Quakers and once the site of their meeting house.

The church of St Peter and St Paul has foundations dating back to Saxon times. The oak table at the back of the church was disguised as a deed chest for many years until the sides and bottom were knocked out to reveal a communion table dating back to Cromwell's time. The box pews were placed in the church in 1842. There is a 14th century stone effigy at the back of the church.

In 1986, work was completed on the reframing and augmentation of bells from four to six, the oldest dated 1638 and newest dedicated to the memory of a former resident of the village, Lady Eastwood in 1985. The work in connection with the bells was a DIY effort by ringers and villagers and was awarded first prize in the Nottinghamshire Village Venture Competition of 1986. New bell ropes were purchased with the prize money, but these mysteriously disappeared after ringing in the New Year in 1988! Oxton had first won this competition in 1979 with the community effort involved in saving the village school from closure. Unfortunately, the school closed in 1984, but has since reopened as a private kindergarten. The exterior is little changed from when it was built in 1870. The first village school was endowed by Margaret Sherbrooke in 1783 and the Church of England school benefited from her charity until its closure.

Through the changing years, and although no longer an exclusively agricultural village, Oxton still retains its country customs and charm.

Papplewick 🦎

Papplewick lies seven miles north of Nottingham, with a population of around 600. Half of the village is designated a conservation area. Meadows and woodland areas with a multitude of footpaths are to be found. One of these provides access to Newstead Abbey, now owned by the Nottingham Corporation and once the home of Lord Byron.

The centre of the village has no village green but consists of a village pub, a garage and the village institute. The last shop, which was also a sub-post office, closed in the 1970s. However, the garage is thriving and was developed from a blacksmith's business.

A great deal of interest centres around what is known as Castle Mill. In the 18th century, children were brought to work here from as far away as London to weave cotton. They were housed in small lodges nearby and many are buried in the local churchyard. The power to drive the machinery was generated by water from the dam adjoining, fed by the river Leen from Newstead Abbey lakes. The mill itself ceased to operate around 1830 but has now been converted to living accommodation, and the dam is no longer in existence, the sluice gates having been demolished.

The church of St James is located at the end of a long drive out of the village and has a very extended history. It has a 14th century tower and inside there is a musicians' gallery. There is a village squire's pew with its own fireplace. Legend has it that when he decided the sermon had gone on too long he would bang the fire irons, which was the sign to the vicar that he had had enough! Electricity was only installed in recent years, candlelight once being the only illumination and on occasions it is still used. The magnificent yew tree in the churchyard is reputed to be nearly 400 years old.

Papplewick Hall is the most outstanding building and was first occupied in 1787 by the Lord of the Treasury and built by the Adam brothers. The local cricket team presently play on a pitch adjoining the Hall which was made available to them by a later squire.

Papplewick is at the southern end of Sherwood Forest and along a footpath leading into Newstead Abbey grounds, it is possible, with permission of the owner, to see what is known as Robin Hood's Stable. This is a cave where it is said Robin kept his horses, possibly in readiness for a foray into the city of Nottingham.

Just outside the village is a splendid Victorian landmark much better known now than in early years. The Papplewick pumping station has

Main Street, Papplewick

been lovingly restored by a group of enthusiasts in their spare time. It was originally built in the 1880s to supply water to the city, but it is not now part of this system as it has been overtaken by modern technology. The buildings and equipment have been preserved and are still to be seen in all their Victorian glory. The station 'steams' at designated times, usually at Bank Holidays and attracts many visitors.

The geology around Papplewick has played a very significant part in its 20th century development. Things could have been very different. In 1919 a landing strip was laid out for RAF training with a proposed development for a full scale aerodrome. Excavation work, however, revealed that ground conditions were unsuitable. Hucknall aerodrome, two miles away, now the site of Rolls Royce engine testing, was the revised location.

Perlethorpe

The village is situated on the Thoresby Hall estate, a community created to house workers on the estate. The original Hall was built in 1683 for the 4th Earl of Kingston but was destroyed by fire in 1745. A few years later the house was rebuilt in Palladian style but this was demolished in the 19th century. The 3rd Earl Manvers found the house too small and so commissioned Salvin to build the present Hall in neo-Tudor style, which took from 1864 till 1875. The entrance tower is modelled on that of Burghley House. The Hall is surrounded by the largest park in Nottinghamshire situated within Sherwood Forest. Because of the likelihood of subsidence damage, Thoresby Hall was bought from Lady Manvers in 1980 by the National Coal Board. It has, however, been resold in 1989 to an Australian Company who intend to convert it into a luxury hotel.

The church was also built by Salvin in 1876 and there is a memorial to the 3rd Earl on the north wall of the chancel. Lady Manvers at the beginning of this century ordered that she should be informed if any child failed to attend Sunday school. She then visited the child and if they were ill would arrange for fresh dairy produce and hot soup to be sent daily until the child was well again.

The lake at Thoresby is one and a quarter miles long and starts from the river Meden at Budby. Ice from the lake was used in winter to preserve game. One year the ice was so thick that a large piece was taken to the Hall for the Earl to inspect. It was about 18″ thick and was placed near the mounting steps at the Hall entrance and remained for several months before finally melting.

The largest wood on the estate is known as The Big Wood and it stretches the full extent of Thoresby Park, east to west.

Workers on the estate were involved in many jobs keeping the hall and estate houses in good repair and providing fuel for the fires. There were large stocks of timber so there was a wood yard and saw mill. Alongside was a joiners' shop where skilled men and apprentices made wooden window frames and panelled doors for farmhouses and cottages. There is a memorial headstone in Perlethorpe churchyard to one of these joiners, shaped in stone with the appearance of rounded wood and showing the tools of his trade. The hall had its own house joiner who maintained the woodwork of the building. There were also wheelwrights, plumbers, painters, blacksmiths, general labourers and a steamroller driver in 1921.

They had their own workshops and tools were kept in the tool house. Some travelled from other villages such as Ollerton and Edwinstowe.

Home Farm was managed by a farm bailiff and cows were reared for milk, cheese and butter to provide fresh daily supplies. The Old Mill, powered by a water wheel, was used for grinding oats and corn for cattle food.

After the Second World War the estate changed rapidly and the small village of Perlethorpe was altered with the building of new properties. The land was also changed and more of the estate was ploughed and turned into rich arable land producing barley, corn, oats and sugar beet as well as grazing land for cattle and sheep.

The village post office still remains the only shop on the estate despite the increase in the population.

Pleasley Hill

Pleasley Hill today is in the District of Mansfield. It is a long narrow area bounded at one end by the river Meden, which at this point is not only the District the Mansfield boundary but is also the county boundary with Derbyshire. Thus Pleasley Hill is only just in Nottinghamshire. On the other side of the river is the old medieval village of Pleasley, joined to Pleasley Hill by a bridge which, until recently, carried the main Mansfield to Chesterfield road. Today, however, the river flows through a culvert under a new bypass.

The 1864 Ordnance Survey map shows that Pleasley Hill was then no more than a collection of buildings confined to a very small area immediately around the bridge. Few, if any, of these buildings remain. A directory of Nottinghamshire dated 1882 describes Pleasley Hill as a small hamlet. However, around the turn of the century a coal mine was sunk in Pleasley and to accommodate the workers, many of whom were redundant colliers from the Staffordshire coalfield, a number of long terraces of small houses were erected on the Nottinghamshire side of the river. These went up the hill along one side of the main road towards Mansfield and they, together with a church, form the major part of Pleasley Hill today. The area of the original hamlet is now usually referred to as Pleasley.

The colliery is now closed, as is also a large textile mill on the Derbyshire side of the river and because of this there is now no large employer in the vicinity. The inhabitants of Pleasley Hill will be commuting either to other collieries which are lucky enough to be still working or to other jobs in Mansfield and surrounding districts.

Plumtree 🦋

Plumtree is within the Green Belt and six miles from Nottingham on the A606 Melton Mowbray road. It has a population of about 200 and lies in an area partially bounded by the former Midland Railway line, now used as a test track because of its unusually tight curve. Despite recent changes, the village still has a post office, a pub, the Griffin Inn, and a village store. In earlier times the village had a second hostelry, the Farmers Arms; both pubs had farms attached, and the Farmers Arms was a coaching inn for the London to Nottingham coaches (the road through the village being the main turnpike). The old forge is marked with a huge nailed horseshoe and is subject to a preservation order.

Plumtree's parish church, St Mary's, is believed to lie on the site of a 9th century church and is one of the oldest in Nottinghamshire. The present building incorporates sections of Saxon brickwork and has interesting Norman arcading and Norman doorways to its west tower; stone for repairing the tower came from the old Trent Bridge. The interior was extensively restored by Bodley in 1873–5, and this work has recently been refurbished.

The instigators of 19th century building and improvement in the village were the Burnside family; both John and William Elliot Burnside were rectors of the church. Mr W. E. Burnside was particularly active in construction of housing, and his initials, WEB, may be seen on several buildings. The school (1840), the Griffin Inn (1843), the post office (1905) and a farm (1909), all built by the Burnside family, form the crossroads in the village. Mrs Elliott Burnside built a village hall (the Burnside Memorial Hall) to the memory of her husband William and laid the foundation stone in 1921.

Plumtree was formerly an agricultural village made up of families whose names, together with much of the village, have largely disappeared. Only three working farms remain, and where many of the farms and acres were all part of the Burnside estate, now only two farms and a small-holding form part of the estate. These were purchased in August 1988 by the Duchy of Cornwall.

Feast Day was once the highlight of the year. This took place around the beginning of June, with a band and grand march through the village into Normanton-on-the-Wolds to call at the 'Big Houses', and then back to Plumtree and a funfair of roundabouts and swings.

Plumtree had a working windmill, situated at the top of a hill, which was owned by the licensee of the Griffin Inn, who was also a magistrate. One day in the early 1900s two young men from nearby Ruddington were before him in court for being drunk and disorderly, and he imposed a fine. The windmill was burnt down within a week, and it is thought that this was carried out for revenge. The mound can still be found in the field.

The railway station was closed in the 1960s, and has since been converted into a restaurant. There is a filling station/motor showroom on the outskirts of the village. Plumtree telephone exchange serves a large surrounding area. It was opened in the year of 1958. Plumtree cricket club is over 120 years old, and over the time it has bought its own ground. In 1988 a new pavilion was built with the aid of members' labour.

Rainworth 🦝

Rainworth, pronounced 'Renoth' by the locals, is a mining village. Rufford pit, at its centre, was sunk in 1911, although Blidworth pit which is older is only a mile up the road.

The development of the village was due, wholly, to the pit. The First and Second Avenues up 'White City' were originally built for the sinkers followed by the 'Model Village' up Python Hill for its miners. Post-war, the Wimpey estate was added off Warsop Lane and the two 'Geordie estates' as the miners from the North East moved south looking for work in the Notts coalfield. The village's brick church, dedicated to St Simon & St Jude, was built in 1983 and a Roman Catholic church was erected around 1960.

Rainworth Water, a series of lakes and streams, is continually being argued about as walkers, naturalists and fishermen fight to keep an area of natural beauty. Joseph Whitaker, a well known naturalist, established his bird sanctuary there and Mansfield Museum houses his fine collection of stuffed birds. The secondary school built on Warsop Lane was named after him.

At the Robin Hood public house the road from Mansfield divides and one road goes to Kirklington and the other to Southwell. Rainworth has a small garden centre and a few shops, including a fish and chip shop which enjoyed being in the limelight in the early 1980s when the notorious 'Black Panther' was caught by their customers. Rainworth made the national news when a shopkeeper at nearby Mansfield Woodhouse reported to the police that a man had been loitering and acting suspiciously. The local police had kept surveillance and in the main street at Rainworth he suddenly realised they were following him. He shot at them, injuring one, but the customers in the fish and chip shop saw what was happening and between them apprehended him. Although even the police did not know it at the time, he turned out to be the much hunted 'Black Panther'. He was wanted, and later convicted, for murder in the West Midlands.

Rampton ✎

The Rampton of the late 1930s was a very different place from the Rampton of today. In those days some 300 people lived in the village, today there is twice that number. It used to be both home and workplace; now few people work in the village.

The village used to provide work for almost every family. The men were mainly in agricultural work on the eight farms then in Rampton; now there are only three with about two men working on each. Apart from the permanent agricultural work there were seasonal jobs for the women and children – many remember 'potato picking' holidays. All the farms had livestock and milking herds; today, not one pint of milk is produced in the village. One farmer had a milk round, selling milk in the district from churns perched on the boot lid of his car. Cream and skimmed milk could be bought from some of the other farms, even on Sunday afternoon.

The village also had three poultry farms, one of which, Mill House – opposite the school – had a windmill, albeit derelict. Fruit and vegetables could be obtained from any one of four flourishing market gardens.

Today, everyday needs are catered for by the one village store which is shop, cum newsagents, cum off-licence, cum filling station cum garage. On the opposite side of the road is the post office.

In what was the bustling heart of the village, Laneham Street, was once the village post office cum general stores. A few years earlier this had also been the village brewery. Opposite was the newsagents' shop and at this time the newsagent was also the tailor. Next to the post office was one of two village butchers; this one was Olivants, run by two sisters and two brothers – all unmarried. They sold meat around the district from a horse-drawn waggon. After buying meat one could pick up some milk next door at Cleveland Farm before going on to the Royal Oak, one of the village's two public houses. Suitably refreshed one could then cross the road to Mr Quickfall's butcher's shop to buy some of his famed sausages and pork pies. Now villagers are dependent on the mobile shops for meat.

Should you wish to have new bread or tea-cakes, Crawford's bakery would provide them. This part of the village always had the tantalising smell of baking bread hanging over it. Mr Crawford also provided the very necessary service of recharging batteries, essential in those days if you had a 'wireless'. The Eyre Arms, the second public house, was next door to the bakery.

Other aspects of everyday life were taken care of by several more flourishing businesses. The cobbler mended shoes and nearby the black-smith made and repaired all manner of metal goods, as well as shoeing the horses used on the farms. There was a garage with petrol pumps near the blacksmith's to cater for the few who at that time had a car or other motor transport. Broken cartwheels were mended at the wheelwright's shop and even up to the late 1950s his wheel template could be seen set into the pavement. Man's final journey was taken care of by one of the two joiners-cum-builders, one of which was the undertaker. Rampton also boasted two haulage contractors.

The village was visited by two local doctors, from Newton and North Leverton, and a surgery was held three times a week in the newsagent's house. They also had their own resident midwife.

In those far-off days Rampton had some of the best recreational facilities in the area. There were flourishing cricket, football and tennis clubs which all did well in the local leagues. There was no better occupation on a warm summer's afternoon than watching cricket in the park. The village hall, or the 'Hostel' as it was known then, was always a hive of activity.

Ranby 🦋

Earlier this century there were between 30 and 40 houses and farms, spread out in an area of one and a half miles square, straggling along where the Retford to Worksop and the Ollerton to Blyth roads merged for about half a mile before going their individual ways. There was a mission church, a blacksmith's and a wheelwright's, a very small post office and food store, an inn cum farm and a village school. The latter had acted as a chapel before the mission church had been built.

The Chesterfield Canal runs parallel with the roads, which cross it at one point with a hump-backed bridge. Nearly all lived in tied cottages working for their respective employers: farmers and owners of the three large houses in the area, Ranby Hall, Ranby House and Morton Hall. This made it a close knit, friendly place, although scattered and without a central focal point such as a church or squire. In the late 1920s, by the generosity of Sir Albert Bingham, it had acquired a good village hall. This has now been taken over by the council and is much in demand.

As in many places change came with the Second World War. The old 'gentry' died off. The Hall is now a burnt out shell, Ranby House is a preparatory boarding school and Morton Hall was knocked down and a modern house built on the site. Roman coins were found, years ago, on this estate.

The surrounding farms became more mechanised and Chequerhouse Farm was razed to make way for the new bypass of the A1, and A614, cutting off the village from the modern motorway. The blacksmith's and wheelwright's became a builder's. The small amount of farmland attached to the inn was sold and the crewyard and cowsheds made into a car park and beer garden. The tied cottages were no longer needed and could be sold off, the buyers making two and three of them into one larger modernised residence. The row of privately built rented houses and the row of council houses were also sold to new incomers and sitting tenants. The fields near the inn were also developed and six bungalows for pensioners were built, a new school was built in the corner of a field way off the road behind the houses, and the old schoolhouse made into a residence. So now the population has trebled that of 70 years ago. There is one telephone kiosk, although nearly every house has its own. With hardly any employment in the village now this means that nearly everyone commutes to business in the surrounding towns.

A mile away a disused aerodrome of the First World War, used as an army camp in the Second World War, was made into a modern prison.

The only organisation, apart from the Brownies, is the WI and the village no longer has the unity of old. But it is still a pleasant place in which to live. The canal no longer transports coal and corn by horse drawn barge, but is popular for pleasure boating and there are still some anglers coming from the nearby towns to enjoy the tranquil surroundings. All the gardens are always trim and the surrounding woodlands and fields well husbanded.

Ravenshead

Three small hamlets, namely Fishpool (so called because of the 'pools' that used to lie along the Blidworth road), Larch Farm and Kighill, gradually merged and in 1966 the village of Ravenshead appeared on the map. The name Ravenshead appears in the Domesday Book and refers to a small wooded area along Blidworth Way.

As houses began to spring up in the 1960s, the population increased dramatically. A small precinct at Milton Court augmented the original Fishpool Co-op and post office and now the village has its own health centre and dentist, a library and many shops. Three village schools, Abbey Gates, Martin Roe and Pilgrim Oak, serve primary and junior chldren. The Martin Roe school was named after the vicar who founded the original school in Blidworth in 1847.

In 1968, the Princess Alice, Countess of Athlone, grandmother of Mrs Abel Smith who lives in the village, laid the foundation stone for the village hall, on land owned by the Garden Society. This is the heart of the village but, as Ravenshead grew it could not cope with local needs, so the Cornwater Barn on Longdale Lane was converted for badminton and became the 'home' of the youth community.

Events have taken place here, both famous and infamous. In 1966 a hoard of gold coins was found in a garden and must have heralded the start of serious gardening for the residents! The Bessie Shepherd Stone on the A60 marks the spot where in July 1817 Bessie was murdered as she walked from Mansfield to Papplewick.

The 7th Lord Byron wove his love of his home into his poems. Newstead Abbey is set in magnificent parkland with formal and informal gardens and a series of lakes. It was bought by the Byron family in 1540 after the Dissolution of the Augustinian priory. The famous Pilgrim Oak Tree at the entrance to Newstead Abbey gave refuge to the pilgrims as they rested along the Packman's Way en route to the priory.

Stroll around the village and you will see many lovely gardens. Along Chapel Lane see if you can spot the evidence of John Slaney's unfortunate death and the Ebenezer chapel, believed to have been the smallest chapel in Nottinghamshire.

Rolleston

Rolleston appears to be a typical Nottinghamshire village – one long winding street with houses either side, a village inn, an open and pleasant prospect and above all a fine church.

Yet Rolleston is rich with unanswered historical questions. At the time of the Domesday Book Rolleston had at least three manors. The Neville manor existed certainly in 1271, until the late 16th century; the old manor was actually pulled down a century ago but two stones carved with the Neville coat of arms can still be seen on the manor house farm buildings. In the centre of the village stands the base of a cross; carvings suggest coats of arms. A manorial meeting place or medieval market site perhaps? The road leading from here to the church encloses what used to be the village green, complete with stocks which have now unfortunately disappeared.

Many villages have beautiful churches but the Holy Trinity at Rolleston is surely one of the finest. The interior is late 12th century, with 13th century north and south aisles; the single lancet at the east end and the 14th century west end circular window are quite unusual. A rare treasure is a portion of the original paper register, made up of 40 leaves stitched together covering the years 1584 to 1615. Completed by the then vicar Robert Leband (who unfortunately drowned by falling into a ditch whilst

Kate Greenaway's Cottage, Rolleston

going about his pastoral duties) his notes tell of current events, local gossip, price of corn. One wonders what event led him to write 'Do not trust a woman not even if she bee dead'!

The local pub, The Crown, dates from around 1832, and was famous for a large tree, the 'horseshoe tree' which had an opening through its trunk, sufficiently large to admit the passage of one or two people. Indeed, after a church ceremony it used to be the custom of the newly weds to further publicise their married state by going through this arboreal archway.

Kate Greenaway, known worldwide for her delightful drawings of children, spent much of her childhood in Rolleston, in a small red brick house. Indeed she often returned in later years to gather inspiration from where she had been so happy as a child.

The majority of villagers in Rolleston still farm the land. There is a peaceful acceptance of the countryside's steady pace, not even affected by Southwell racecourse, which borders the boundary between Rolleston and Fiskerton.

Ruddington 🎄

Ruddington is a commuter and industrial village of approximately 7,500 residents and is situated five miles south of Nottingham. The name is derived from 'Rudda', a Saxon headman.

It once housed many hosiery workers and a number of high-windowed houses belonging to the framework knitters remain.

It has the usual amenities but especially important are its three museums. One houses a unique hosiery workers' complex; one in the old school has old farm implements, an old fish and chip shop, a chemist's shop of the early 1900s and an old cobbler's shop, also a Victorian schoolroom; the third housed in The Hermitage, a very old house, has a Victorian drawing room, a library of old books for reference and various artefacts unearthed during an archaeological dig. The 'dig' took place at Flawforth churchyard, two miles east of Ruddington and took 20 years to excavate. Many items of antiquity were discovered, some dating back 4,000 years.

An interesting tree stands half way between the village and Flawforth church, called 'the Resting Bush'. This was the spot where villagers carrying coffins from the village for burial at Flawforth would stop and rest from their heavy burden.

The village boasts a well cared for village green, three churches, Anglican, Methodist and Baptist, and there are seven public houses.

Until the 1980s parishioners celebrated Rogation Sunday by processing to the fields to ask for a blessing on the crops and on Ascension Day choirboys mounted the church tower to sing hymns in the early morning. On St Peter's-tide the village Wakes took place and a service was conducted amongst the roundabouts.

Ruddington is proud to be still a self-contained village protected by a Green Belt and residents would fiercely defend attempts to encroach on it. It is an independent and friendly village and has absorbed many newcomers who are actively supporting various organisations.

Screveton

Screveton is a small farming village of approximately 100 inhabitants, on the edge of the Vale of Belvoir, situated one mile from the Fosse Way.

Screveton, meaning 'farm of or belonging to the sheriff', is pronounced 'Screveeton' or 'Screyton' by the older inhabitants and 'Screeton' by newer ones.

Half a mile from the village, secluded behind a field with access by footpath, is the church, dedicated to St Wilfrid, its Feast Day being held on the Sunday before St Luke's Day, the 18th of October.

This small 13th century church, set in a pretty churchyard, is interesting from the variety of its style of architecture. There is evidence of an earlier church on the same site. In the choir are two miserere seats beautifully carved, one being 'winter'. A man on a settee sits warming feet and hand at a fire, with a book in his other hand. The other seat is of the patron saint.

The principal family in Tudor and Stuart times was the Whalleys. An alabaster tomb in the church under the carved royal arms of King Charles II, is of Richard Whalley in armour, feet resting on a whale, his three wives and 25 children kneeling. His third wife Barbara, erected this tomb to his memory, one of the finest in the country.

On the village side of the church is the Priest House, a listed building, showing herringbone brick structure. A seven foot high pinfold is in Lodge Lane, where any stray farm animals can be housed. There is a manor house, Old Hall dated 1702, three 17th century cottages with dormer windows and cottages with brick and pantile roofs.

Since the 1920s there have been three generations of Willis's at the smithy. Horses were shoed by Alexander (Alec) Willis until 1985. On Sunday mornings local men queued to have their hair cut by him at the blacksmith's shop. Three sons continue smithy work in mechanical engineering, wrought ironwork and welding.

Three generations of the Marsh family have farmed here. There are five arable farms, sized between 100–250 acres, being in each family for approximately 50 years. Recently three lots of barns were made into a restaurant and two homes, and the old chapel school converted into a house.

Two woods were grubbed out because of Dutch Elm disease. During the last 50 years eleven cottages and a reading room were demolished and three bungalows and one house built. In 1960s eight council bungalows were built for elderly villagers.

In the 1950s Harry Derry used to tend his beast on the wayside and Stan Clarke would fetch his cows for milking, herding them through the village. Screveton had its own roadsweeper who kept the village tidy.

Miss Alice Bean was a village character. She lies in the churchyard alongside her many brothers, who all fought in the First World War. The only girl, she spurned marriage on her wedding morning because she couldn't leave her brothers to fend for themselves.

Screveton is without mains sewerage and its landscape is marred by a line of huge electric pylons. Yet Screveton and Car Colston are the only villages near the Fosse Way without street lighting.

Scrooby ❧

Scrooby, skirted by the river Idle, is best known for its Anglo-American ties as it was the home of the Pilgrim Fathers. It even has a village pub called after them. William Brewster became the postmaster at Scrooby in 1587 after leaving Cambridge University. His duties included delivery of mail, providing a change of horse and bed and board for travellers.

Along with his good friends Rev John Robinson and William Bradford, they developed the Puritan principles. They held meetings in the outbuildings of his house but his beliefs were to lose him his job and he was replaced in 1607. It was not until 1620 that the *Mayflower* departed for America with 100 people on board – others were to follow. 'Elder' Brewster was one of the leaders of the expedition, answering to the name of Aaron of the Exodus.

The Pilgrim Society of Plymouth put up a commemorative plaque on

Brewster's home, Scrooby Manor, which was built on the site of a former palace of the Archbishops of York. Both Henry VIII and Cardinal Wolsey are known to have visited there.

Selston 🌿

Selston is situated on the Erewash border with Derbyshire, eleven miles north-west of Nottingham and five miles east of the Derbyshire town of Alfreton. The Domesday Book says 'there is a church and three acres of meadow' and from earliest times agriculture was the main occupation, but beneath the soil lies coal, indeed, no less than 16 seams outcrop at the surface within the boundaries of the parish.

For centuries it has been populated by folk who worked the land either above or below ground. The original lease for coal dates from 1206 and for generations carts of grain from the Trent valley were exchanged for Selston coal. Initially the mine workings were shallow and small-scale but, with the coming of the Nottingham to Newhaven turnpike and the development of canals and railways, deeper shafts were sunk and the pace of industrialisation in the parish increased. By the 1850s Selston had taken on the aspect of a modern colliery village.

Alongside agriculture and coal-mining, ironstone mining and framework knitting provided employment from time to time. Frames were expensive and were usually hired from the large warehouses like Brettles of Belper and Morleys of Nottingham. The work was demanding, the hours long and the wages scandalously low and most families were obliged to put their children to learn the trade from the age of six or seven, the boys winding the yarn on to the bobbins and the girls learning seaming from their mothers.

Ironstone mining is still commemorated in the local place name of 'Toadhole', which was derived from the toad-shaped nodules of ironstone found in the vicinity of the old workings. The last Selston coal mine, the 'Bull and Butcher', closed in 1956. Few of the old colliery structures now remain and many of the old shafts have been excavated, filled or capped. The old pit tips have now disappeared or have taken on new shapes and appearances by contouring, seeding and the planting of trees and shrubs. The dominant source of employment within the village nowadays is in the clothing industry where the workforce is mainly female, and only on a small scale. Selston today is virtually a commuter village. Sadly, the closure of the pit saw the passing of a way of life where strong-knit family and community ties created a neighbourliness and caring concern that we may never see again.

In 1879 John de Morgan, who was described by *The Independent Police Review* as 'this unflinching champion of freedom', became involved in the villagers' struggle to retain their rights to common land. Meetings of protest were organised, but the patience of the people wore thin and soon there were reports of trespass on enclosed land, the removal of crops and the destruction of fences. In all, two and a half miles of fencing were destroyed. As a result 26 men were arrested and tried, first at Mansfield and then at Nottingham Assizes. The vicar of Selston appeared in court and gave a good account of the general conduct of the accused men and they were eventually bound over and dismissed. De Morgan and Mr William Peach, a local worthy, were flung into prison at Holloway. When 'Old Billy' was released he was accorded a hero's welcome from the village. De Morgan had captured the hearts of the people and his name will live on in Selston.

The beautiful Norman church of St Helen commands a fine view out to Crich Stand and the Derbyshire Hills. In the children's corner stands the Norman font, which has had a curious history. Some 200 years ago it was removed from the church and taken to Blackwell. It was returned to Selston, but strangely, not to the church but to the Bull & Butcher Inn where it was fixed to the pump. Later it served as a flower pot in a private garden and from there was rescued by the Rev Charles Harrison, the then vicar of the parish who, in 1906, restored it to its proper place.

The neatly tended churchyard with its beautiful trees is the last resting place of one who travelled far. Here lies Dan Boswell, the king of the gipsies. For many years the gipsies would return to Selston to pay their respects and new-born babies were all brought to the church to be baptised. The words of Dan's epitaph are scarcely legible now but they have been remembered by the village folk.

> 'I've lodged in many a town,
> I've travelled many a year,
> But death at length has brought me down
> To my last lodging here.'

Shelford ✺

Shelford lies in the valley near to the river Trent, taking its name from 'the place of the shallow ford'. The Domesday Survey in 1086 noted

Shelford and at that time it had a church and priest and population of 250 persons. Its population today still stands at about 250 people.

Seen from the Malkin Hills the view today is still one of the prettiest in the area. As one descends into the village there is the impression of an almost unchanged quiet backwater.

Although quiet now, Shelford has had a turbulent history, featuring strongly in the Civil War. On one November weekend in 1644 a cruel battle took place at the church tower when Royalist soldiers were smoked from the tower by Parliamentary soldiers setting fire to straw and a whole garrison of approximately 200 men were slaughtered at Shelford manor house. Later the beautiful house was burnt to the ground by an unknown hand.

A fragment of a Saxon stone cross found in the buttress of the south side of the church of St Peter and St Paul, suggests that the lovely church which is situated on the edge of the village with views over the Trent, stands where people have worshipped for nearly 1,000 years. The massive Perpendicular tower is a feature of the church and forms a conspicuous landmark in the valley of the Trent.

Farming has always been a mainstay of the village and still is today. There are six farms in the village and one on top of the Malkin Hills. In the past many villagers were employed in the osier beds, cutting and stripping the willow, which was then baked and dried and sent on to the various areas where basket weaving flourished. Today only a small area of willow bed can be seen near Shelford manor. Today's villagers still farm, but most new residents commute to nearby towns and cities to work.

The village owes its quiet atmosphere to the fact that the Earl of Carnarvon, who sponsored Carter to find and open the Tomb of Tutankhamun, died, so it is said, from the curse laid on all who opened the tomb. Upon the Earl's death, Shelford and considerable tracts of land which had belonged to him, passed to the Crown, who to this day still own the land, thus protecting Shelford from the large scale development which has changed other small villages.

Shireoaks

Twice the recipient of a Best Kept Village award, Shireoaks gets its name from an ancient oak which once cast its shade into the three shires of Yorkshire, Derbyshire and Nottinghamshire. John Evelyn, the diarist, described the tree as being 94 feet round and covering an area of 700 square yards. Both the river Ryton and the Chesterfield Canal flow through the village.

The Hall and its land were once owned by the Hewitt family. One of them, born at the Hall in 1656, became known as the 'Notorious' Sir Thomas, because of his avowed atheism and rakish, eccentric behaviour. He commenced the building of a marble mausoleum to house his pagan remains but died before it was completed. Legend has it that his servants tried to foil the relatives' plans to have Sir Thomas buried in the parish church of Wales, a nearby village, by stealing the body from the coffin and replacing it with stones. While carrying the coffin at night through Scratta Wood, a sudden strong wind blew out their torches, and thinking this was an omen the frightened bearers returned to the Hall and replaced the body in the coffin, which was duly interred in Wales church. Scratta Wood, said to have been haunted, has since been uprooted and burned, and is now under cultivation.

After a period of disuse the Hall is again occupied, and the owner is making progress with plans to build a restaurant on the estate. The two ponds in the park are a pleasant venue for fishermen.

Farming still flourishes in Shireoaks, mainly in the production of arable crops, and one farm rears a prize strain of Friesian cattle. The mill ceased to be used for grinding corn in the early part of the century, and after being used for a number of industrial purposes, has now been converted into a private residence. A reminder of its original use is the two mill stones in front of the building.

In the late 1850s coal was found and a pit was sunk, eventually bringing employment for up to 600 men. Expansion over recent years, has been followed by present day threats of early closure.

The church of St Luke at Shireoaks may not yet qualify for recognition as an ancient building, but few churches in the country can claim connection with so many people and events of historic importance. The money for the building of it was given by the 5th Duke of Newcastle after the sinking of the pit, when he also built a long row of cottages for the colliers. In 1861 the church's foundation stone was laid by the Prince of Wales, later King Edward VII, and consecrated on St Luke's Day 1863. When the east windows were inserted, Mr Gladstone, then Chancellor of the Exchequer, came to dedicate them. A banquet was provided in a marquee, and guests were entertained by music played by bandsmen of the Sherwood Rangers regiment.

The spire of the church, a notable landmark, was removed in 1975. It had become unsafe due to mining subsidence and structural problems.

The tower supporting it was retained and roofed over, and re-roofing of the church has recently been completed.

The Steetley Company, now internationally known, began its operations in Shireoaks and still has its Transport Division in the village. For their employees, Steetley Sports Field is a delightful venue. Bowling and football are also popular on the Miners' Welfare field. A piece of waste land has been transformed into a village garden by members of the Women's Institute and is a pleasant place to meet by the riverside on a sunny summer day.

The old vicarage is now a small residential home for the elderly, and the village has a post office, general stores, butcher, fish and chip shop, hairdresser, newsagent, garage and public house – services few villages can boast of at the present time.

Skegby

In the 17th century a group of Quakers met regularly at the Skegby home of Elizabeth Hooton. She was a Quakeress of distinction, bearing the title 'First Minister in the Society of Friends'. Members of the society were regularly summoned before the Justice of the Peace for holding their religious meetings.

In 1870 the Parish Church of St Andrew was completely restored, such that nearly every trace of its Norman origin has disappeared. Coal mining caused subsidence to appear and girders had to be used in the restoration. Even to this day the church is still affected by subsidence. The Old Vicarage situated in the croft adjoining the church was also badly affected and had to be demolished. An entry in the burial register at St Andrew's dated 27th April 1869 shows that Joseph Cooksey was buried aged 38 'drowned by water in Molyneaux Pit along with three others'. This was as a result of a colliery disaster on 20th April, 1869.

St Andrew's Church of England Primary School, formerly the National School, was built on land given by Lady Carnarvon in 1865. The school was opened on 31st July and an entry in the Master's Log Book for 17th August states 'Lady Carnarvon, Mrs Morgan, and the Rev. & Mrs Taverner visited today. Her Ladyship was so pleased with the singing, the conduct and the general personal appearance that she promised them all a bun.' At that time 95 children were on the register but attendance was not, at that time, compulsory. The only master for these 95 pupils was William Barlow.

Skegby has a particularly fine example of a Cruck cottage on Old Road dating from about the 14th century. The rarity of this particular cottage was not discovered until it was being renovated in the 1950s. Another property of interest is Dalestorth House. Built in the 18th century it is of Georgian design. Dalestorth House has now been fully restored to its old world charm. Today it serves as a guest house at the crossroads of the Sutton-in-Ashfield bypass road.

On Mansfield Road there is a well restored Pinfold or Pound. This is where stray animals were kept until the owners reclaimed them after having paid their fine for allowing them to stray. In 1967 a hoard of 450 sterling pennies were discovererd on a building site in Mansfield Road. They were dated from the reign of Edward I and declared treasure trove.

The village has now grown much in size though much of its old world charm has been retained. Stone walls, cruck cottage and the pinfold preserved. The site of the old railway line has been turned into nature walks allowing long neglected (or forgotten) wild life to return.

South Clifton ❧

South Clifton is a pleasant Trentside village midway between Newark and Gainsborough, with Lincoln twelve miles to the east.

Coalyard Lane winds to the old wharf where coal from Yorkshire and Derbyshire used to be off-loaded from barges and carried by horse and cart to customers over a wide area. Traces of the wharf and bollards used to secure ropes are still visible and the 'basin' into which the river can overflow remains in use. Power-driven barges carrying sand and gravel between Notts and Humber ports came later, still taking advantage of the tides. This stretch of the Trent has always been popular with fishermen but in these days they have had to come to terms with the water skiers.

A 17th century house, once the Boat Inn, stands high above the river, out of danger of the many floods that occurred down the years.

The floods in 1947 were the worst in living memory and people had to be taken to and from their homes in boats. Marks were scored on some of the walls to show the high water level. After this, extensive work to raise and strengthen banks was put in hand and earth was excavated from land on the south side of Clay Hill. Ancient bog oak was found and also antlers, said by experts to be 8,000 years old. The huge hole left was fed from a stream and became an irrigation pond for farm fields. Trees planted all around it and in other low ground nearby, attract various kinds of wild life now. An archaeological dig on a field to the east of the village yielded flints, coins and other signs of an early settlement.

Dominating the village from the west side of the Trent are the five cooling towers and buildings of High Marnham power station and the suspension footbridge, built for its personnel only.

The first Wesleyan chapel, built in 1814 and later used as a Sunday school and then tea rooms, still stands, adjoining Ivy Cottage on Front Street. In 1882 a new chapel was erected and is still used, a section of the north end having been partitioned off in 1934 for use as a schoolroom and vestry. The beautiful little church of St George the Martyr just over the boundary in North Clifton, serves the Anglican community from both parishes.

Two octogenarians still living here remember when the population included eight farmers, a carrier, baker, boot and shoe maker, threshing machine owner, saddler, bulb and geranium growers, joiner and wheelwright, builder, publican, shopkeeper, blacksmith, butcher, resident policeman, postman and at sometime a miller, but the mill had become unsafe to be worked. The blacksmith's shop was sited on the south green and round it the children used to play 'tin lurkey', a kind of 'tag' using the back of the shop as the base for the tin. During severe winters there was ice-skating on the river and in summer cricket matches on the marsh, with the annual gala known as Clifton Feast in September.

In 1981, on the green where once the blacksmith worked, a young oak tree was planted, with a plaque to commemorate the achievement by local farmer 'Dusty' Hare of the highest number of points ever scored in Rugby Union Football. Dusty, who has lived in the parish all his life, went on to score 7,000 points and was awarded the MBE in the 1989 Honours List.

The farms are still worked, with fewer men and larger machines but the old crafts and trades have gone. For a time there was a garage. A new market garden and nursery was founded in 1944 and still operates.

South Muskham & Little Carlton

South Muskham and Little Carlton are small villages sharing the same parish, about a mile apart from each other and two miles north of Newark. The villages are divided by what was once the Great North Road, before the arrival of the Newark bypass.

South Muskham has a mention in the 1086 Domesday Book. The village church of St Wilfrid stands at the east end of the village and from inside can be seen Saxon, as well as Norman, masonry. The village has no pub, but it's a pleasant walk to the nearest inn at North Muskham. With about 90 dwellings in the village its character and charm is retained within its boundaries of lakes that were once gravel pits, the railway line and the Old Great North Road. Little Carlton on the other hand is aptly named so as not to confuse it with the larger Carlton-on-Trent. It is a village of 40 or so dwellings straddling a country lane, and within its boundary there is a cricket pitch, which was kindly given to the parish by local farmers.

Farming has played a large part of village life here, but gone are the days when you could see shepherds driving their sheep across roads and fields. Most fields are now sugar beet for the large factory, one mile away towards Newark, and apart from rape seed and winter wheat as alternative crops, few fields are still given over to sheep grazing. This had led to disused farm buildings being converted to residences. Now both villages are under threat of over-development.

Mr and Mrs Cooper have perhaps seen all changes in South Muskham over the last 80 years. From the sale of village land and property to local people and residents, through to seeing the houses we now live in, being built on what was once arable land. The local village hall standing prominently on the corner, being paid for by funds donated by a local farmer and villagers. The closure of the one roomed village school, which also served as the village hall in days gone by – people can still remember their school days there or when functions were held. Not to mention the many other goings-on that have changed out of all recognition the villages that once boasted 12 or so houses between them. Today Mr Cooper has many a tale to tell, like when as a schoolboy, he and a friend went to see if there were any eggs in the nests at a nearby orchard. The boys scooped up the eggs and hid them under their flat caps. However, as no good comes to those who are up to mischief, justice was only around the corner in the form of the local bobby on patrol on his bike. 'Hello,' he said and gently tapped them on their heads. Their misdeeds became then all too apparent!

Southwell 🐛

Southwell nestles in a valley, whose surrounding small hills protect and shelter it from the severest of weathers. There are many natural springs, streams and wells in the vicinity but the location of the actual well from which the name was derived is unknown. Southwell has evolved from five hamlets, namely the High Town, Easthorpe, Westhorpe, Burgage, and Normanton, into a thriving busy community without losing its individuality.

The magnificent Minster overshadows Southwell. Its spires of lead and Rhenish caps, known as 'pepper pots', can be seen when approaching from any direction. The Minster takes most visitors by surprise, as Southwell does not seem large enough to accommodate its presence. As the Mother Church of Nottinghamshire it is the centre for many religious festivals and civic services. For as long as the Minster has been in existence a school has provided education for the choristers. The Minster is not the only place of worship as there are other denominations, each with its own individual history and buildings, those of the Methodist and Baptist churches dating back to the 1800s.

Within close proximity to the Minster there are many fine buildings to be found, among which are former prebendal houses, each impressive in its own right. Equally imposing is the Saracen's Head Hotel, the oldest inn in Southwell, where Charles I stayed just prior to his surrender in 1646. There are also 18th/19th century cottages with a charm all of their own. It was in the garden of one of these cottages that the now famous Bramley apple came into being. The Miss Brailsfords propagated, from pips, the original tree, part of which is still in existence. Commercial growing from cuttings taken from this tree was undertaken by Henry Merryweather and the Bramley apple is still one of the finest cooking apples in existence today.

Most of the varied small businesses and retailers are to be found in King Street and Queen Street. It is in these streets and the market square that exchange of conversation takes place and the coffee shop is aptly named 'Gossips'. The narrowness of these streets can cause a little congestion on busy days but the inhabitants prefer it this way.

Many different types of now defunct businesses, including the making of baskets, lace, cheese, silk and rope, provided employment in the past. A brewery, tannery and a flour mill were also part of the local industry. Reminders of these past businesses are shown in some of the street names

147

Cauldwell's Flour Mill at Southwell

– Hopkiln Lane and The Ropewalk. History is also recorded in other street and house names recalling past connections with the town's benefactors and this practice is continuing today.

Away from the hustle and bustle there is an expanse of green with mature trees. This is known as the Burgage Green. Interesting properties

148

that surround this area include Burgage Manor, where Lord Byron's mother resided. Just below the police station is the former entrance to the House of Correction. Built in 1807 this was the local prison and housed petty thieves. Among other items of interest are the Victorian letterbox and an old water pump.

Permission would not be given by the authorities for the construction of the Nottingham to Lincoln railway line through Southwell. Whilst this prevented industrial development, the absence of heavy industry helped to preserve the historic buildings. Later in the 19th century a railway line was built and this conveyed passengers between Mansfield and Rolleston on the train affectionately known as 'Paddy the Push and Pull'. After the closure of this line the council developed it into a nature trail and it is only one of the 70 footpaths to be walked in this lovely rural area.

As with most rural areas there have always been agricultural and horticultural shows but to meet the demands of building developments the venues of these have had to be changed. This also applies to the golf and race courses and whilst the golf course has never been replaced, the racecourse is now firmly established at the neighbouring village of Rolleston, but still retains its identity as Southwell Races.

Stanton-on-the-Wolds 🐝

Stanton-on-the-Wolds lies in south Nottinghamshire on the edge of the Wolds. The Nottingham to Melton Mowbray A606 road runs through part of the village, which has a population of 450.

There are no shops, post office or public houses; the mobile library visits fortnightly. The children have to go to Keyworth's Willowbrook primary school, although it is stressed that this is still in Stanton parish. The same applies to the Roman Catholic church: the school was built in the 1960s and the church in 1985.

The parish church of All Saints stands in a field and is reached by a footpath between farm buildings. It is one of the smallest churches in South Notts and dates back to the 11th century. It is built mostly of boulders, some of them from the Fosse Way.

There is a fine 18 hole golf course. At one time there was a water tower, which could be seen from afar, but sadly that was knocked down in 1985.

Stanton is in the Green Belt, mostly agricultural. In the 1960s there were seven dairy farmers in the village, now there is not one.

Stanton has had various names: from Stanture of 1086, to Estanton in 1235, and Stanton Super Wold in 1240–80. It is said that in the late 18th century the village was devastated by a freak storm when huge hailstones smashed roofs and cottages, and this accounts for the absence of really old buildings.

Staunton-in-the-Vale 🌿

This attractive village in the Vale of Belvoir lies on the borders of Nottinghamshire, Lincolnshire and Leicestershire. Only one mile from the village stands the Three Shires Bush, planted where the three counties meet.

The village consists of about 20 dwellings, an inn – The Staunton Arms, historic Staunton Hall and a church situated next to the Hall grounds. The Hall is the home of the Staunton family today, as it has been for centuries. The village is particularly attractive in spring, with cherry blossom bordering the drive to the Hall and church, the Hall grounds abounding with daffodils, scillas and aconites and the church-yard a veritable carpet of primroses.

The land surrounding the village is part of the Staunton estate and is mainly farmed but the land is also rich in minerals such as gypsum, which until comparatively recently was mined in the village. The land has now been restored to farming but a factory is still in operation for the manufacture of gypsum products – the ore being mined from surround-ing areas. There are attractive walks in the village, particularly in the area of the park, which is flat grassland bordering onto mixed woods.

Staythorpe 🌿

Staythorpe is a small hamlet of three farms, only one of which is still a working farm, and 20 houses. It is situated on the road from Averham to Rolleston, close by the Newark to Nottingham railway line.

It was mentioned in the Domesday Book, when it was called Startorp. Staythorpe later belonged to the monastery of Newstead, but when Henry VIII dissolved the monasteries he gave the land to Trinity College, Cambridge. The farms belonging to monasteries were called 'Grange Farms'. In Staythorpe the Grange is now called 'Manor House' but the Grange Farm is still called by that name. It was a coaching inn and reputed to be 300 or 400 years old. In the 18th and early 19th centuries it was a public house called The Durham Ox.

In 1946 there were great changes when a large area of land was sold to the Derby Electrical Co and Grange Farm, together with a small parcel of land, was sold to Mr Phillips – after 400 years it had become a privately owned farm.

The building of Staythorpe power station was started in 1946 and the first unit was put into service in March 1950. Thirteen houses were built in Staythorpe for power station staff by 1950, which greatly increased the size of the village. Another larger power station was commenced in 1956 and was officially opened in May 1962 though it had been running for quite a while then. The first or 'A' station was decommissioned in 1983 and demolition was started in 1986 and finished in 1988. The power station houses have now been sold to people who commute to neighbouring towns for work.

Sutton Bonington ❧

Sutton Bonington lies in the Soar valley, just near the point where Nottinghamshire, Leicestershire and Derbyshire meet. In the manner of many villages of the area, it is a long straggling settlement, the more so because it unites the former hamlets of Sutton and Bonington. The most conspicuous features inherited from the past are the Hall, a fine Queen Anne mansion, and the Manor, a Victorian house which replaced a decaying Tudor building. There were two huge rectories (one still occupied by the rector, the other used for offices and accommodation), two churches, three pubs, two chapels and seven shops.

The other prominent feature of the village is Nottingham University's School of Agriculture, founded in 1895 as the Midland Dairy Institute. Its beautiful campus is the academic home of between 400 and 500 students, many of them from overseas.

Like so many villages of the area the local economy was based on agriculture and framework knitting. It is astonishing to discover that in the middle of the 19th century there were as many as 50 workshops making stockings here. As this traditional craft declined (the last surviving workshop can be seen in the garden of 80 Main Street), and agriculture became more mechanised, new employment opportunities arose with the railways (whose line crosses the village), with the corn and spinning mill at nearby Zouch, and with the famous brick and pot works known as Hathernware. Now, there is only one working farm left in the village and though the School of Agriculture employs many local people, most people commute to work.

New events, fast becoming traditions, have been established in recent years, and perhaps the most popular is the 'Garden Walkabout', which is held on the last Saturday and Sunday afternoons of June. Villagers are invited to open their gardens to the public, to raise money for charity, and between 30 and 40 families usually respond. On other weekends the very attractive grounds of the Hall and the Manor are also open for charity, so Sutton Bonington has something of a reputation for its gardens.

A reputation of a different kind is attributed to a former resident, Mr W. Tate, who was headmaster of the village school from 1926 to 1933. He was passionate about local history and introduced the subject into the school syllabus. Later he wrote *The Parish Chest*, which is still a standard work for local historians. Later in life he became a lecturer in Historical Studies at Leeds University, and was regarded as 'one of the most important agrarian historians of the century'.

Another village character was Mr William Riste, who died at the age of 30 in 1773, and who was known as the wonderful Nottinghamshire Giant as he grew to be 7 feet 4½ inches high. His hands and limbs were equally gigantic and he was viewed three times by the Royal Family. King George III presented him with a suit of scarlet silk.

On the main road, next to the school, is a large stone house, probably late 17th century, known as Hobgoblins. Its stone arch and walls were built from stones of the old Repingdon Grange, which had belonged to the priors of Repton for over 350 years. There seems to be no evidence for the popular belief that a secret tunnel connects it to St Anne's church, but its claim to be haunted appears to be more substantial. Locals claim that a ghost/being/spirit can be heard climbing the stairs, indeed, some have given detailed accounts of actually hearing the footsteps on the stairs.

Sutton-cum-Granby

A mile to the east of Granby lies the quiet little hamlet of Sutton-cum-Granby. Although it has been in existence for over a thousand years, perhaps it is one of the few villages which has seen very little change in character and life-style.

Lying in the shadow of Belvoir Castle, Sutton once possessed its own castle. Not a 'grim fortress' but classified more as a moated homestead to which the villages could withdraw in troubled times'. Traces of the moat still remain visible in one of the fields. Sutton has experienced little in respect of modern house building, but many of the old dwellings of mud and stone were demolished at the beginning of the 20th century as being unfit for habitation. There were times when as many as 500 people lived here whereas now the number is down to 57. Most of these villagers are engaged in farming.

At present Sutton has no shop or public house. But it does have a chapel, which is undoubtedly one of the smallest in the country. It measures 18 feet square and the door opens right onto the village street. When it was built in 1860 it had no organ. Hymns were sung unaccompanied with sometimes disastrous results. Someone in the village possessed an old harmonium which was loaned for services but the owner would not allow it to be left in the chapel, 'lest someone broke in and meddled with it'! So it was carried to the chapel every Sunday evening for service. In time this grew rather wearisome, so an organ was purchased for the sum of £8 10s. This was in 1920 and it is as good today as ever it was.

Sutton-cum-Lound

On each approach to this sprawling village the 15th century pinnacled tower of the parish church (dedicated to St Bartholomew) is to be seen overlooking the village. The older parts of the chancel are 14th century and a tall arch on massive pillars unites the chancel to the nave. An old oak chest and an ancient alms box are of great interest. Tradition has it that one chest was used by the Archbishop for his chalice, as an identical chest is in York Minster. Some very interesting bench ends are fashioned in many shapes, one being known as the 'Queen of Sheba'. The first entries in the oldest register were made by James Brewster (vicar 1594–1614), presumed to be a brother of William Brewster, one of the Pilgrim Fathers.

No lord of the manor has lived in Sutton since the Archbishop of York used it as a residence in the 12th century. Old Sutton House (renamed the Manor House) was demolished and the present house was built in 1892. The second small manor was the Rectory Manor.

Trades in the village used to be many and included a miller, a wheelwright, two bootmakers, one schoolmaster, two publicans, a builder (who collected taxes), one higgler (a barterer of goods) and a blacksmith, among others.

The windmill stood to the rear of Mill House, as did the bakery – a necessity in those days, bread being the staple food of the villagers. The oven was made of brick with a sand-filled cavity above, which served to keep the oven hot. Faggots of wood were used to heat the oven; when they had burned out the embers were removed and afterwards the oven cleaned with a wet cloth on a long pole. It was then ready for baking a batch of loaves.

Georgian cottages stand next to modern houses. One 18th century cottage, the former post office, stands beyond the Gate Inn which has served travellers for many years. Originally three chapels existed, but only one today remains in use as a Methodist chapel.

The modern Church of England school replaced one built in 1781 and which was situated on the Sutton–Mattersey road between the two villages of Sutton and Lound.

A legend reveals a haunting at the Sutton crossroads. In 1692 a rider returning by horse from taking a sick maid home, saw something white which seemed to spring out of the ground, running alongside her horse, leaping up behind and she felt a cold arm around her. After a brief time it vaulted from her horse, disappearing back into the ground. Records state that a man named Will Brumble had hanged himself at that spot in March 1672.

Life in Sutton today bears little resemblance to those early days. Across the road from the church the old smithy is now a workshop for a new business. Many inhabitants of Sutton commute to nearby towns which offer various positions in trade and industry. Numerous fund raising events are held in the village hall, the ground for this building being a gift from the Duke of Portland in 1936. One colourful sight which is a great attraction, is when the local hunt meet in the village once or twice a year.

Sutton-on-Trent 🦢

Sutton-on-Trent, 8 miles north of Newark on the A1, almost certainly owes its existence to the proximity of the river Trent, where early settlers found water, fishing and good farming land. The 13th century church, with its beautiful early 15th century oak screen, was built on Saxon foundations on one of the few areas of high ground in a large flat area.

Over the centuries the river has changed its course, but the settlement remained and prospered.

As expected, the main occupation of the bulk of the population was farming of all types and even as recently as 1965 there were 18 farmers and smallholders operating locally. The village has also been famous in the past for basket making, especially baskets for fishermen. This industry employed many men (and women) in the late 19th century – workers coming from all over the country, one even born in Pittsburgh, USA!

The Great North Road was eventually re-routed away from Sutton, thus relieving the village of heavy traffic and congestion – but it has also become a barrier to extensive development to the west. Thus, with the river to the east, building has been contained and the main street plan varies little from early days. Apart from the church there are no really outstanding buildings, although the windmill, built about 1830 on the site of an earlier one, and derelict for years, is now being restored as a private dwelling.

Sutton is fortunate to have within its boundaries over 300 acres of grazing land bordering the river. These are known collectively as The Holmes, the area being divided into 'Cattle Gaits', the ownership of which gives entitlement to grazing according to strict rules. Numerous people own these rights, some handed down through generations, others more recently acquired. At an enquiry held by the Commons Commission in 1985 the Public Trustee was established as the owner of this land and the County Council was appointed as trustee for it. Every spring the custom of Gait Letting takes place in the village hall. Here farmers and other interested parties gather, and the gaits are auctioned in lots of varying size. Successful bidders are entitled to graze cattle, according to the number rented, at the rate of one beast per gait, from May until December.

The life of today is obviously very different in many ways, but Sutton still retains its village atmosphere and there is a pervading feeling of good neighbourliness. A programme of controlled housing development has meant that it has not lost its old character.

The Trent valley power stations are a large source of local employment, together with other old established firms and individual businesses operating from a small industrial site.

As an example of the community spirit prevailing, the village Church Restoration Association was recently set up as a registered charity. It is a purely non-sectarian organisation whose members and helpers belong to

155

all denominations – or to none at all – and is dedicated to the repair and restoration of the church building. So far over £15,000 has been raised, and much pleasure provided for many hundreds attending its various functions.

Syerston

One local resident remembers village life as it used to be before the Second World War. 'There were no famous people in the village, but some who had considerable local acclaim! There were people whose jobs have now gone forever: a "length man", a ginger-moustached little war veteran, whose job was to tidy a length of the Fosse with a stiff yard brush and a wheelbarrow.

'The village had just moved into the Electric Age, but many still had lamps, using paraffin, sloppily dispensed with a pint jug from a huge open metal barrel by Mr Vear.

'The church was candlelit too, two candles on a T-shaped support to every other pew; and a glowing solid-fuel stove under the floor. We did the laundry in rainwater and drank the pump water. The rain-water collected was delightfully soft, and wonderful when clean; but in dry spells it could turn bottle-green and harbour wildlife, which had to be strained out. It was hard work keeping clean, and I remember being told, "No respectable girl needs more than one bath a week!" The bath water was heated in the copper, or in a bucket hung over the open fire.

'We had a laundry in the village. It's a house now, but in those days it was just like the one described by Zola in *Nana* – wooden scrubbing tubs, wooden-rollered mangles, pulley-airers, and a special stove to heat the flat irons, Italian irons and goffering irons. This was a special laundry and expensive. Rich people from far away brought their laundry for expert service.

'Although quite a few people made their own bread and several had a cow or goat, one lady at least used to take butter and eggs, fruit and poultry into Newark by horse and trap, and several took produce by bus into the shops: flowers, wild flowers, blackberries, wild rabbits: and twice a week the baker came with his horse-drawn, iron-tyred bread cart. The butcher came twice a week too, with a high-stepping bay in a high-wheeled trap. But the joy of the week was Lunn's Shop, a van with roll-up sides, which came on Fridays and sold everything.

'Another bygone professional was Jack the Thatcher. He made a lovely

156

job of thatching the stacks, with a plaited ornament to top each one. Not allowed to smoke, he chewed twist and could spit on a bluebottle from six feet away.

'We had a travelling blacksmith. His smithy has gone, but it was a Badge of Courage for the children to crawl in through the window and get a horseshoe nail to wear as a trophy.

'Great events? Well, we had the Caravan Mission occasionally, a marquee in a field with a fervent preacher and a harmonium; a change from church and chapel (we children went to both, for a good sing and a warm and a meeting with friends!).'

Teversal

Teversal village has been described in local guide books as an 'oasis set in an industrial wilderness'. The first Anglo-Saxon church (made of wood) was mentioned in the Domesday Book. Being a manorial village it was centred around a very beautiful manor belonging to the Molyneux and Carnarvon families, the local public house being called the Carnarvon Arms after the family connection.

The school was part of the estate and was first held in the tithe barn but the last school, which was donated to the village by Lady Carnarvon, is now two private residences. Lady Carnarvon took a very keen interest in the schooling of the local children and was a frequent visitor to the classrooms. She was remembered especially for her visits in the autumn when, accompanied by a man-servant wearing livery, she would deliver a hamper of apples from her orchards. The children would line up and with a curtsey or a bow, receive two apples – one cooker and one eater – which were usually consumed on the way home.

The church itself is steeped in history, especially its rare set of hatchments. These are panels bearing the coat of arms of deceased persons and they are said to be one of the finest sets in England, dating from the 17th century. There is also the beautifully carved Carnarvon Pew, decorated like a four-poster bed with handsome cushions and books. Pews for the servants and pages etc are situated at the back, as was fitting in those days. The Molyneux underground crypt is another unusual feature of the church. It is approached by twelve under-pew steps and it contains twelve leaded coffins, thought to be members of the family from 1653. This crypt is rarely opened to the public.

Teversal is also the fictional home of D. H. Lawrence's Lady Chatter-

157

ley and the woodlands neighbouring onto Hardwick Hall estate are reputed to be the meeting place of her and the gamekeeper. These woods are a delight in springtime with violets, wood anemones and drifts of wild daffodils. Hardwick Hall is one of the homes of the Devonshires and Lady Spencer's Walk (who was once imprisoned there) is a lovely small valley. The southern side is now an estate of what were once colliery houses, which were the result of two colliery shafts being sunk. One is still mining coal but the other has now closed. Until then, and now to a large extent, farming was the main occupation.

The smithy and the chestnut tree at the crossroads have disappeared due to road widening but memories still linger of seeing the coal carter's horses being shod, farm waggons being welded, children's scooters being repaired, hoops being straightened and 'lad-lassing' around the chestnut tree. It was also on these crossroads that the toll-bar was situated alongside the village pub. Many travellers would pay their toll and pause for a drink en route from Mansfield market to Tibshelf. This was also the corner where the town crier could be heard.

The village at one time boasted two railway stations, used for passenger, mining and other goods traffic. The station houses are still inhabited and the unused tracks are being converted into nature trails which are of particular interest to the conservationists, as rare bushes and plants are found along its banks. A neighbouring meadow with wild orchids, mosses, lichen etc is hopefully to be kept with a preservation order, as only a handful of such meadows are now to be found in the county.

Life continues in much the same way, a few houses have been discreetly added and cars have taken the place of horses, but the violets and wild strawberries can still be found.

Thorney

Thorney, first mentioned in the Domesday Book, is a small village which is situated twelve miles north of Newark. There are about 350 inhabitants, with no village shops and apart from a post office and a parish church no other facilities. The church was built in 1846, the earlier Saxon church having been pulled down due to its inadequate size for what was expected to become a growing village. It is built on a Norman design with some of the masonry having been imported from Italy. The new church was originally commissioned by the Rev Christopher Neville who lived at Thorney Hall, for an approximate cost of £80,000. This well-meant project eventually brought financial ruin to part of the Neville family, who now no longer live in the village.

Thorney has no murky past apart from an incident which is said to have taken place on the outskirts of the village near Drinsey Nook on the 3rd November, 1805.

A navvy by the name of Thomas Temporell and known locally as Tom Otter, was forced into marriage to a Mary Kirkham of South Hykeham, whom it was claimed he made pregnant. He was so upset by this accusation and enforced marriage, that he murdered her on their wedding night in a frenzy and so it is said, put the remains of her body under the steps of the Sun Inn public house at Saxilby in Lincolnshire.

Otter was eventually sentenced to death in Lincoln by the Grand Jury on 12th March 1806, together with the extra penalty of 'gibbeting' (a gruesome custom of hanging the body of the offender in chains at the site of the murder – presumably as a deterrent for other would-be murderers). Otter was duly hanged outside Lincoln Castle on 14th March and his body returned to the toll gate vicinity, where it was gibbeted on 20th March 1806.

Locally, the B1190 Doddington road is known as Tom Otter's Lane and a piece of woodland close by is called Gibbet Wood. It is still rumoured that if you go there at midnight you will find traces of blood on the road and could well meet the ghost of Tom Otter!

Thrumpton 🦋

Thrumpton was originally called Turmodeston. The small settlement of wattle huts and small houses was at first inside the present park of Thrumpton Hall, near the old drive that came from Ratcliffe-on-Soar. It was not until the end of the 17th century that John Emerton enclosed the park, building new houses round the church. Mr George Seymour, the owner of the Hall has really made it his life's work to keep all the part of the old village which still belongs to him, as lovely as it was.

The village had a very good choir in the 19th century and often sang in Southwell Minster. This was due to Lucy, Lady Byron, who lived at the Hall until 1912. All her servants had to have good voices to get their jobs!

She had the old church restored by Street and this also gave employment. Sadly the old double pulpit was destroyed and the old font is now in the churchyard.

Mrs Grundy used to live in the old Ferry farmhouse. She was famous for her outspokenness on morals and what one should or should not do. She was in the service of George III. This house was to have become a public house but Lucy, Lady Byron got together with the Cliftons and other ladies of manors in Ratcliffe, Kingston and Normanton and to this day there are no pubs.

Samuel Chettle was a great character of the village, having started as a little boy scaring birds off the crops for Samuel Plowright of Barton. He became a farm worker, a great lover of horses, and for many years kitchen gardener to Mr and Mrs Seymour at the Hall. He was very worried that he would have to go to London to receive his long service medal for working for one family (40 years), but the late Duke of Portland came over from Welbeck and did it!

There used to be wonderful Harvest Suppers at Barton and Thrumpton and many people would sing songs, including Sam who was always called on to sing 'I'll be a roving rover no more'. Hardly appropriate as he never was one, but rendered most feelingly.

Like many villages nowadays there have been many changes, as a number of new houses have been built. The families who have come and gone, and those living here at present have mostly enriched the community life. The village has no shop or pub, but the village hall is in great demand for social evenings.

Thurgarton

The settlement or farm of Thorgeirr (an old Norse name) is one of the ancient villages of Nottinghamshire.

In the Domesday Book, Thurgarton appears as one of the 34 Nottinghamshire manors granted to Walter d'Ayncourt who was, by marriage, connected with William the Conqueror. Ralph, his second son, founded Thurgarton Priory about 1140 for the regular canons of the Augustine order (the Black Canons). It is said that one still haunts the priory grounds. Originally the priory was about the size of Southwell Minster. The best known of the canons was Walter Hilton (died here 1395) whose book *The Ladder of Perfection* is still read and valued.

The priory was closed by Henry VIII in 1538. The king gave the buildings to William Cooper and the land to Trinity College, Cambridge,

Beck Street, Thurgarton

the present patron of the living. The church later fell into ruins and stone and timber were acquired by villagers to build and add to their farms and homesteads. Evidence of this can still be seen today.

In 1854 the church was restored by the Milward family. The original stone altar was recovered from a nearby well. Sufficient remains of the church to give a good idea of its former grandeur. The buildings and their inhabitants had a great influence on the surrounding countryside, and in some respects continue to do so today.

A brick Georgian building replaced other stone buildings and in 1884, when the Southwell diocese was founded, the first Bishop of Southwell, George Riddings, lived at the priory. Many people came to the village to go into service there and a few still live here. The priory is now owned by Boots Ltd and used as a research centre. So villagers still find work and worship at the ancient site.

The railway came to Thurgarton in 1846. At one time the station boasted a stationmaster (his house remains), a clerk, two porters and three signalmen. A few years ago an 'open crossing' was installed, to which the villagers protested most strongly. After a battle over some five years, the barriers have been reinstated.

161

Methodism came to the village around 1833. Today church and chapel work together with a thriving Sunday school at the chapel and Youth Fellowship run by both.

Thurgarton has a beautiful cricket ground, overlooked by church and priory. The cricket club (with a woman president) turns out two senior teams and a junior team. It holds an annual six-a-side match with teams invited from other villages, and has supported many benefits for Notts cricketers.

There is a small industrial estate on the far side of the railway and gravel is still being excavated along the Trent valley.

A beck meanders through the village, past the village shop (with sub-post office) where once was the village blacksmith, past the war memorial – once a sheep pen (all the stray animals were penned there), on down Beck Street past the school which closed after a long fight in 1974, built 123 years ago and now converted into a house. Further down you will find the 'Family Greengrocer', another character in the village, the Old Rectory and many old cottages.

The population, in number around 350, surprisingly has changed little over the years.

Tithby-cum-Cropwell Butler 🦢

In the beautiful Vale of Belvoir some nine miles from Nottingham are two adjoining villages, which at the time of the Norman Conquest were named Tithby and Cropwell Butler.

The parish church of Holy Trinity is at Tithby, an Early English building famous for its 14th century font and priest's door, its Georgian furnishings and double decker pulpit. Cropwell Butler has never had a church, although until recently there was a Victorian chapel of ease (1845). The Methodist chapel, rebuilt 1904, has now become the church of Cropwell Butler, shared by Anglicans and Methodists. The children of both villages attend the flourishing Sunday school at the Methodist church.

A notable man, the son of John Smith, a small landowner at Butler, was Thomas Smith (1631–1699). He founded the first of a group of banks whose progressive development has gained the Smith family an honoured place in the annals of British banking. The branch of the National Westminster Bank on South Parade, Nottingham, continues to be known as Smith's Bank Branch.

Butler is the larger of the two villages with about 500 inhabitants. Once self-sufficient, it has several owner-occupied farms, mixed arable, employing local men, and some local industry. Surviving local craft is maintained by a joinery and fitted furniture manufacturer employing about 22 men, many living locally. There is a small business producing frozen sausages, pies and pastry for home cooking from a production unit in the grounds of a large house. A local lady and her daughter deliver daily milk, eggs, cheese and other products from a Vale of Belvoir dairy. A textile designer studio in a listed village house has trans-atlantic connections and landscape design is carried out in another listed house. A post office remains.

Tithby has about 50 inhabitants and remains a mainly farming village. There are two large farms, one arable and one dairy, both Crown Property.

Despite attuning to the needs of the present day, old customs and rites are not forgotten and are practised. One farmer breeds and works Suffolk Punches, another farmer maintains a herd of Highland cattle, and on Plough Sunday the plough is still brought into Holy Trinity church to be blessed. Rogation Sunday is marked by the parish priest, weather permitting, leading the congregation, together with the choir from Cropwell Bishop to the farms for Divine Blessing.

Tollerton 🦢

Tollerton, a South Nottinghamshire green belt village with a population of 2,000, is fortunate to retain two churches, a school, a post office, a restaurant, a garage, four shops, an airfield, six farms and the Hall.

Entered in Domesday Book in 1086 as Troclaveston, it is believed to have originated as a Saxon settlement known as Thorlaf's ton. No early ruins remain, but from the 11th century the manorial lordship has passed through the Barry, Pendock and Neale families, whose younger sons were often rectors of St Peter's church. The best known squire was the eccentric Pendock Barry, who in 1812 started extensive and disastrous refurbishing of the beautiful Norman church and built a covered ambulatory from it to the Hall for his own comfort, also a family pew with red hangings, a family mausoleum and a fireplace which still remains. He quarrelled violently with his cousin the rector, the Rev Pendock Neale, and erected a high wall to blot out the view of the church from his home. He also encouraged the congregation to leave St Peter's for Plumtree church – a movement which has been repeated in the last decade for different reasons.

In 1929 the Hall ceased to be a private house when the occupier, Mrs Burnside, split up and sold much of her land for building, causing the growth of the village. The Hall then became briefly a residential country club where valets and horses could be accommodated. It was next a training college for congregational ministers and during the Second World War was used by the army, the RAF, American airmen and finally as a camp for Italian prisoners of war who worked on local farms. After the war it reopened as St Hugh's College, a Roman Catholic seminary, which closed in 1987.

The Hall has now been very beautifully restored by an insurance company, Bankarts, whose staff enjoy the 120 acre estate which includes a lake, fed by the village stream and a variety of wildlife.

The oldest houses cluster round the Hall and church and include an ornate archway house which once belonged to the gamekeeper and was used as the post office during the war. The Town End cottages, which border the airfield, housed the first school in an upstairs room when the village population was only 169 in the 1920s.

Too much heavy traffic still uses the village as a short cut despite the newly opened bypass. Otherwise Tollerton is remarkably rural for a village which is only five miles from Nottingham. Most residents work in Nottingham or Leicester. The airfield only caters for small, light aircraft and helicopters except on the occasions of the one or two air shows each year.

There are a few small workshops on the fringe of the village and Wheatcroft's famous roses are within smelling distance, both when there are acres of them in bloom and during the muck spreading season!

Trowell 🌿

Trowell was first mentioned in the Domesday Book as Torwell, which means 'well at the top of the hill' – in fact about 15 wells have been found in Trowell. The Domesday Book also tells us that 'It had a priest and half a church and six acres of meadow all valued at 20 shillings'. Trowell was a Saxon settlement in the 10th century and has certainly grown and altered since then. Through the years Trowell has been owned by the De Trowells, the Willoughby family who built Wollaton Hall, and their descendants, the Middletons.

In 1881 the village had 421 inhabitants, an increase of 151 over the previous census figure due to an influx of workers from the Black Country, who came to work at the forge which was established in 1870. A new station was opened at Trowell in 1884 which meant that people could more easily travel from the village.

In 1851 people's occupations were listed as cordwainers (shoemakers), a starchmaker, coal higglers, and a washerwoman. Coal was dug on Trowell Moor as early as the 13th century and there was a colliery on the Trowell border employing quite a few men until 1926. The other industry which made such a difference to life in Trowell was the Iron Co, now known to everyone as Stanton and Staveley Co. There were two forges in Trowell where blacksmiths could be seen at work and a water mill was on the river Erewash – still known as the 'Boards'.

Life in the village in the old days was very hard. The old forge cottages were classed as the poor part of Trowell and the area round the church as the 'better off' part. There was one tap to every six houses and an outside toilet that had to be emptied every day! An old resident, Annie Page, recalled how during the winter, water was fetched from a spring in the corner of the field but when this dried up clothes were washed in the canal and drinking water fetched from the Ely Well. The milkman brought milk in a churn. A paraffin man delivered oil for the lamps until electricity came in the 1930s, and a road sweeper with a hard brush cleaned up the village.

Trowell had some beautiful buildings and although modernised, they are still very picturesque and full of character today. One cottage was the old pub, The Ring of Bells. Opposite the church is one of the oldest houses in the village, Rectory Farm, originally Trowell Hall, owned by a well known County family, the Hackers. Along Trowell Moor are some lovely cottages, two of which are the old workhouse where the homeless were given shelter. Another beautiful place is Trowell Hall, where villagers were entertained to tea after helping with 'beating' for the shoots. Waterloo Cottages were built in 1815.

The oldest building in Trowell is of course the beautiful old church, St Helen's. Remains of an old Anglo-Saxon church have been found in the chancel, which dates from the 13th century. The church has a square embattled tower containing six bells which are still rung every Sunday. It has a clock which came from the demolished Exchange Buildings in Nottingham in 1927.

Trowell today has altered a lot but still holds on to some of its old landmarks. The three old pubs have all gone. The Ring of Bells is now a

165

pretty cottage and the Barley Mow was pulled down a hundred years ago because of a dispute over a bowls match! In 1956 the Festival Inn was opened but was a far cry from the old village pubs with its bars and a dance hall! At this time the M1 was built and two cottages were demolished to make way for it. The village was gradually filled with modern houses and now a new estate stretches along the Trowell border. There is a modern village hall and an excellent village school built after the old Church school, which had served the village for generations, had proved too small and inconvenient.

Trowell was chosen as Festival Village for the Festival of Britain in 1951, because of its mix of industry and rural life, and because it was just about in the centre of England.

Underwood with Bagthorpe

Underwood and Bagthorpe form part of the extensive parish of Selston, situated eleven miles north-west of Nottingham and five miles east of the Derbyshire town of Alfreton. The parish lies on the exposed coalfield and from the Middle Ages, though farming was the main occupation, coal was mined here. Throughout the centuries other pockets of industry, ironstone mining, framework knitting and the manufacture of bricks, have provided employment. With the construction of the Nottingham to Newhaven turnpike and the coming of the canals and railways the pace of industrialisation quickened as the sharp rise in population during this period would indicate. Today most signs of that industrial activity have disappeared, and the area has become part of a commuter belt.

The two villages are a study in contrasts. Underwood stands on high ground. Bagthorpe on the other hand, shelters below, its secluded, wooded valley dipping towards the lowest terrain in the parish. This is an idyllic spot, where scattered farms and homesteads straddle the meandering brook. Fortunately for Bagthorpe folk it still lies in the green belt. May its drowsy tranquillity long continue.

High on a neighbouring hill stands Underwood. It was in 1879 when the shaft of an earlier pit was deepened and rows of terraced houses were erected at Pit Row, Palmerston Street and along the Main Road, that it took on the appearance of a typical 19th century colliery village. Though sadly the pit has now closed, it still retains the stamp of a mining community. The headstocks now stand in the churchyard, a lasting tribute to the miners and their womenfolk who spent lives of drudgery and toil. Their sacrifices should not be forgotten.

Just off the Mansfield Road, its Elizabethan chimneys glimpsed among the trees, is Felley Priory, now a private residence. Once an Augustinian foundation, it was established in 1156. On a hilltop site overlooking Bagthorpe, stand the ruins of Wansley Hall. This was, according to the Domesday Book, one of three manors in Selston. There was once a chapel here and, so local legend has it, an underground tunnel. Wansley and Felley had connections going back to the Middle Ages.

The oak-shingled spire of St Michael and All Angels in Underwood dominates the countryside for miles around. Built of grey stone in the Gothic style the church was erected by Earl Cowper in 1890. Sixty years before this, Bagthorpe Baptists, awaiting the completion of the baptistry in their chapel, were accepted into the faith by immersion in the brook.

In recent years, as a result of strenuous and lengthy campaigning by local stalwarts, Underwood has acquired its own doctor, a truly splendid complex of sheltered housing and a community centre. This, the churches, the Miners' Institute and the six 'locals' provide venues for some lively and enjoyable social activities.

The dialect of the Erewash valley is quite distinctive and, although much of it has been lost, many local people cling to their familiar ways of expression. 'Aitches' and the definite article seldom feature in their speech. They 'mash' tea and wash 't'pots'. Rain 'siles dahn', they eat 'taters' and 'nobby greens' (Brussels sprouts); when they are 'starved' they are cold, not hungry and until recently every miner greeted his mate as 'sorry', his version of the Elizabethan word 'sirrah'.

Mummer's plays were a feature of life in the area until the Second World War. Dressed in bizarre costumes and with blackened faces, local youths with a pretended show of force, would gatecrash Christmas gatherings in houses and pubs to re-enact the age-old story of the triumph of life over death in Nature, the origins of which go back beyond pre-Christian times. Over the centuries the performances had become pure knock-about farce. However, there existed an instinctive respect for their antiquity and no door was ever barred against the Bullguysers. Unfortunately, to safeguard the blackout in the war years, the police had to insist that the Mummers should play no more and another age-old custom was lost.

Through his friendship with Jessie Chambers (Miriam of *Sons and Lovers*) who taught in Underwood School, D. H. Lawrence knew the

167

countryside around this area and loved it intensely. In a letter written in 1926 he expressed his appreciation of its beauty thus:

'If you're in those parts again, go to Eastwood, where I was born. Go to Walker Street and stand in front of the third house and look across at Crich on the left, Underwood in front – I lived in that house from the age of six to eighteen and I know that view better than any in the whole world – that's the country of my heart.'

Upper Broughton 🦢

Upper Broughton nestles attractively into a steep hillside on the borders with Leicestershire with, from its eastern boundary, extensive views across the Vale of Belvoir. The brook which marks the county boundary is only a short distance; a good place to search for fossils.

Certain maps denote the village as Over Broughton but in earlier times it was Broughton Sulney. The entry in Domesday Book shows that Broton or Broctton was the land of Aluredus de Suleni, a Norman, but the title Broughton Sulney is nowadays used only for ecclesiastical purposes. There was once a Roman settlement here.

The ancient church of mellowed sandstone, at one time St Oswald's, is now dedicated to St Luke. The oldest part is a fragment of an arcade from Norman times in the south aisle. The nave is 13th century, the central arcade, tower and font 14th century. Old fragments are built into the 18th century porch. The churchyard contains some interesting 18th century slate headstones.

The 18th century chapel, originally the mother church of Baptists in this area, is also at the eastern end of the village.

In a field by the brook is the Woundheal Spring, the waters of which were said to be beneficial for scurvy.

Many cottage buildings are of attractive local brick and some maps show the site of the old brickyard along the Hickling Lane. In a field alongside the same lane stood the windmill, the site of which can still be discerned by way of a grass mound. The pleasant Mill House still stands at the entrance to the village.

The village has two greens; one is a lovely sight in springtime with chestnut and birch trees and a mass of golden daffodils, planted by the Women's Institute in memory of Miss Dowson, the village's first WI President. The daffodil named 'Upper Broughton' has a pure white circular perianth and the small pink crown has an attractive eye and a band of deeper pink. The second green contains the remains of an ancient cross which is said to commemorate deliverance from the Black Death. Nearby is an interesting lead cistern dated 1777 ornamented with the signs of the Zodiac.

The main occupation of the villagers for many generations was farming. There are now fewer farms in existence but Manor Farm has the fine Sulney Herd of pure British Friesian cattle. Former farm buildings have been tastefully converted into pleasant dwellings.

The region is well known for the production of Stilton cheese and pork pies. Cheese was once made in the village but this practice has long since ceased. However, excellent pork pies are still produced in quantity, as they have been for over 80 years, by a village family firm.

Bernard Pearson Hayes first came to England during his service with the Anzac Forces in the First World War. He returned to New Zealand but eventually he and his wife settled in Upper Broughton in 1947. He dedicated his life to the service of the community and did much to improve and maintain the well-kept appearance of the village. He had a great love for young people and when, greatly as a result of his efforts two all-weather tennis courts were erected, he devoted much of his time in coaching young people in the game.

Cricket has been for many years and is today a favourite weekend sport for players and spectators. Apart from the teamwork of cricket and tennis, the village has an active Sunday school. The restored village hall provides for many occasions and one event looked forward to with anticipation is the annual Art Exhibition. There is a general store cum post office, greengrocer, butcher, and a regular visit of a well stocked mobile library.

Following a strenuous game of cricket or tennis, there is available the local inn, The Golden Fleece, to discuss the finer points of the game!

Upton ✣

As the road from Newark to Southwell rises from the flat fields of the Trent river valley, Upton comes into view on its little hill. At first there is a glimpse of the nine-pinnacled church tower standing above the trees and rooftops and then suddenly the traveller has arrived. No gradual entrance here, for Upton is a typical Nottinghamshire linear village with its cottages and farmhouses built sociably along the main street and the long gardens and orchards running behind towards the open country. The architecture is traditional brick and pantile, warm and friendly;

there is a small green with thatched post office, telephone box and village seat. A peaceful country scene? Not quite, for the road is busy and has been an important highway for many years.

When the new Archdeacon of Newark, Francis West (later Bishop West) became vicar of Upton in 1947, he arrived in the large old vicarage during one of the coldest winters in living memory. Post-war fuel shortages and power cuts encouraged most people to retire early to bed; the vicar was no exception but, scholar and great reader, he used the time to examine the 17th century churchwarden's and constables' account books he had found in the ancient parish chest. What he discovered amongst those laboriously inscribed pages threw a completely new perspective on ordinary life during that most turbulent period, the Civil War; two years later he published *Rude Forefathers* and opened a door through which it was possible to step back over 350 years.

The Upton of 1641 was not very different in size and shape from the modern village, though the cottages were considerably more primitive and the Hall and vicarage a fraction of their present size. The rising land around the settlement was farmed in three great open fields, and the areas sloping to the river were used for grazing and flax-growing. The village fortunes were reviving after the disastrous plague of a generation before, when sufferers had been banished to huts by the Newark road – an early

The Post Office, Upton

170

form of the isolation hospital built near the Southwell road this century – but when still a third of the population had died. The account books, recording the daily transactions of the parish, have an entry for 9th February which apparently describes just one more family in the list of poor travellers who could call on the constable to give them food, lodgings and money for the next day's travel from local rates: 'Given to a linen draper of Newcastle which was deprived of all his goods by ye Scots to ye valew of two hundred pounds having a wife and six small children – 4d'!

The story of maurauding Scots was hardly new, but this one was different and heralded the first skirmishes of the Great Rebellion. Less than two years later King Charles I, having failed to rouse Nottingham to his cause, set up a large garrison in Newark: for the next five years Upton was inextricably caught up in civil war.

Upton soon found itself levied by new, Parliamentarian, masters, but when they were absent, parties of foraging Royalists regularly arrived in the village to replenish supplies for the garrison; in desperation now they looted and plundered and eventually murdered. A respected villager named William Robinson was killed trying to prevent his horse being taken, and lies buried in the churchyard. No wonder a look-out was now employed on the church tower, to keep watch all day and toll a warning bell whenever the Royalist troops were seen riding up the road from Kelham. Not everyone feared their arrival it must be said. The redoubtable Mrs Skinner, wife of the alehouse keeper, seems to have supplied drink and hospitality cheerfully and with enthusiasm to both sides.

However, the arrival of the Scots in support of the Parliamentarians brought suffering on a large scale. For six months, with no pay and during a winter as terrible as 1947 they lived entirely off the local population. In the spring of 1646, a sad, dispirited King Charles arrived in Southwell, and on 5th May he surrendered himself at the Saracen's Head to an escort of these same Scots. He was brought through Upton to the Scottish camp near Kelham, and ordered the Newark garrison to lay down its arms.

In 1984 the Queen drove through Upton on her way to distribute the Royal Maundy in Southwell Minster, and as her car slowed around the sharp bend by the village green, cheering villagers stood under the tree planted by Bishop West to commemorate her wedding day and waved their flags. Daffodils, blue sky and sunshine, bunting and happiness – how different from that day in May all those centuries before.

Walesby 🦎

Walesby is surrounded by farming land and woodland, on the edge of Sherwood Forest. In the past it comprised several small farms. The menfolk were then able to nip into the Red Lion for a quick drink at one end of the village and into the Carpenter's Arms at the other end. Next door to the Carpenters' was Pashley's Prospect Bakery and all the bread etc. made was delivered by horse and cart. The 'paraffin man' sold his wares from horse and wagon while the blacksmith waited at his anvil to shoe horses etc. The doctor's surgery was held in the front room of a house. There was also a chiropodist, a post office and a small shop which supplied the needs of the village as far as possible. The old school had its own library and it was built onto an old cottage.

St Edmund's church stands at the east end of the village and is a fine ancient stone building. One wall displays the Stanhope coat of arms and it has two fonts – one either side of the door, one of which came from Bevercotes church many years ago. The church used to be surrounded by some majestic beech trees. Sadly, these were felled in recent years without notice. Across the road stands the old vicarage, it is a fine building standing in its own grounds. Many garden fetes have been held in its gardens and the whole village took part.

The scene changes through the years to the present. Today there are only two farms left. Deans Farm Eggs is a big concern which used to be Hempsalls and close by is the International Scout Camp which is known the world over. In 1988, 8,000-plus scouts visited Walesby – near the site is Robin Hood's Cave and the Kings Highway ran straight across the camp to the north. The village had a scout patrol in 1916.

The great majority of the village people commute to work. There are 200-plus pensioners, many early retired residents and also young mums with toddlers. These are the keepers of the village during the day but have no much needed leisure facilities.

Warsop 🦎

Warsop, a large parish, contains several other settlements: Sookholme, Nettleworth and Gleadthorpe. Warsop Vale was built after 1900 to house miners at Warsop Main Colliery. Spion Kop dates from the Boer War period; Welbeck Colliery Village followed the opening of Welbeck

Colliery and a new mining village was added on to Church Warsop in 1926. Because some of its first occupiers worked during the General Strike, it bore for many years the nickname of Scab Alley.

Warsop had always been a small farming community with some quarrying. Part of the parish is magnesium limestone. Warsop lime was supplied for the restoration work at Southwell Minster after the Civil War, and shallow quarrying has left some areas of humpy ground, now noted for birds and wild flowers, called the Hills and Holes. The rest of Warsop is on forest sand. Farming is less easy there, but must have been worthwhile for several areas were carved from Sherwood Forest for cultivation, known as assarts. At Gleadthorpe there is an Experimental Farm for sandland techniques.

The coming of the railway and two large collieries at the start of the 20th century changed Warsop's rural quiet, and it is now a very cosmopolitan place. Quarrying has ceased, there is a little light industry, and some farmers have been largely displaced by mountains of colliery waste.

Warsop is widely known by the saying 'Do you come from Wahsup?' said to anyone who leaves a door open. This is said to derive from the time when the old single-entrance cottages nearly always had the street door open. Some say it was curiosity, others claim that Warsop people have always been very hospitable to strangers.

Warsop's most notable buildings are the churches at Church Warsop and Sookholme with Norman features, the mill of 1757 and the mill dam opposite, and the parish centre made in 1974 from the former manor house. It contains 13th century work and a beautiful Tudor barn.

The village has lost since 1950 a medieval pack horse bridge, an ancient dovecote and an old rectory with a well-authenticated ghost of a Roundhead soldier.

Between Church and Market Warsop lie the river meadows called the Carrs, a beautiful open area which makes a good starting point for many walks towards the woodlands to the east, north and south.

Warsopians have two favourite jokes for visitors; to recommend them to visit Sookholme Docks and The Swing. A small stream at Sookholme had a concrete edging made to keep the water off the lane. At Warsop Vale stands the Vale Hotel; for some mysterious reason it is always called the Swing locally.

Watnall 🦢

Watnall lies seven miles north-west of Nottingham on the B600 road to Alfreton, within the parish of Greasley. There is no church or school in the village and it was originally divided into Watnall Chaworth and Watnall Cantilupe, named after former owners of the land.

Before the Second World War the area was extensively farmed. Some of the larger farms remain, still in the same family, but new buildings now cover the land of those which were actually in the village. In the 1930s the inhabitants worked on the land, at local collieries or at the brickworks; some were employed at the Hall (in Watnall Chaworth) by the Rolleston family, the last of whom were Sir Lancelot and Lady Maud. Lady Maud really was the Lady of the Manor – the boys and men touched their forelocks to her and the girls curtsied. She ran a Sunday school in a small chapel on the estate – the chapel is now the WI Hall.

After Sir Lancelot and Lady Maud's deaths the Hall was sold in 1961 and subsequently demolished. A small housing estate was built on the site and the only reminder of the Rolleston family still left in Watnall is a small railed burial ground in the field behind the site of the Hall. There are other memorials in the parish church at Greasley.

In 1939 the WI Hall was commandeered by the Royal Air Force and during the war years it became a Fighter Group Headquarters. The area surrounding the Hall became an RAF camp and afterwards when the area was cleared a housing estate was built. The village has one shop – the post office and general store – and two public houses, both of which have so far kept their village character. Very few of the older cottages and other buildings remain.

Today, an industrial estate sprawls over what, until coal nationalisation in 1947, was a coal wharf and private railway station belonging to Barber, Walker and Company. This took colliers to pits as far as Langley Mill and brought coal from Watnall Colliery and bricks from the adjacent brickworks, four of whose tall chimneys still dominate the skyline.

There are few people in the area today who know that the Nottingham Weather Centre (Watnall Met Office) stands on what was the village green, and that until 1914 Watnall Wakes were held annually on this site. The main event of the year now in Watnall is the annual Moorgreen Agricultural Show, held on land next to the Queen's Head public house on August Bank Holiday Monday. Many thousands of visitors converge on the village that day.

Welbeck Abbey

Welbeck is the country seat of the Dukes of Portland, and along with Clumber House, Thoresby Hall and Rufford Abbey, is known as The Dukeries in Sherwood Forest. There are four villages on the estate: Holbeck, Holbeck Woodhouse, Norton and Cuckney and it is in these villages that the estate workmen live. There are wood and forestry, farms and works departments, all of which keep in repair the houses and buildings on the estate, all supervised by an Estate Office, based on Welbeck. The Lady Anne Cavendish Bentinck is now the owner of the estate.

It was the 5th Duke who started a vast building programme from 1854 to 1879 and made Welbeck what is is today. He built the impressive riding school, the second largest in the world, with a peat floor and lit by gas jets. He had built the three mile long tunnels which are quite famous, and most of the houses and lodges were built in this time too. When the 6th Duke, who was a second cousin, inherited in 1879 it was really a magnificent estate and the heyday of Welbeck started.

The Duke was a great racing man and he bred and reared racehorses at his stud at Huncecroft in Holbeck, and the world famous stallion, St Simon, stood there. The Duke won many races, including three classics, in one year. From the money from these three races the Duke built a row of six almshouses, and called them the 'Winnings'. These are usually let to widows of workmen who live on their own. The estate had its own school where schoolchildren were provided with cloaks to wear for school, the boys navy blue, the girls red, new ones being provided every two years. When they met the Duke or Duchess, they curtsied. Another tradition was that everyone in the villages kept a pig to be killed in October, ready for Christmas, the pig's fry, pork pies and scraps to be distributed to everyone. Another custom that is now a thing of the past.

There were house parties every weekend, and shooting parties. In 1915 the Duke had built at Holbeck a beautiful new church and called it St Winifred's (his wife's name). It was built by his own workmen and many visitors come to see this, and the churchyard, which contains the family graves.

It was the Second World War which ended this era of Welbeck. The Army took over in 1939, with the parks as a training ground for tanks, and the riding school becoming an Army depot. This lasted until the end of the war.

The Duke died in 1943 and his wife Winifred, the Duchess in 1950. In

1952 the Abbey was taken over by the Ministry of Defence as an Army training college, maintaining the Abbey and grounds in perfect condition. The masters and their wives have added a depth of community to the village life during the years the college has been on the estate.

There are a lot of new people and faces in the villages today. The estate is letting quite a lot of houses now as they become vacant. They have built some craft shops in what was once the kitchen gardens and these are let out to the very finest of craftsmen, these people also renting houses.

Wellow ✑

Wellow is a very pretty conservation village, one and a half miles from Ollerton on the Newark A616 road. It is very well known for the permanent maypole on the village green, and the annual maypole celebrations each May, with the crowning of the May Queen, and the maypole dancing which follows, keeping up the tradition of several centuries.

It was a fortified village, once protected by earthworks on two thirds of its perimeter, and by the Gorge Dyke on the western side. This was for protection from plundering neighbours of the villagers and their cattle, which would be grazed on the village green in the centre of the village, where now stands the maypole. The remains of the earthworks can still be seen.

On the high ground to the north-east of the village, by the side of the wood, there is the outline of the site of the 13th century castle of Jordan Ffoliat, who in 1268, it was recorded, obtained permission to hold a weekly market on the village green and an annual fair.

From the 12th century, when the Cistercian abbey was founded by Gilbert De Grant, Wellow always had close ties with Rufford, and an uneasy relationship existed with the Abbot and the monks. After the Dissolution in the 16th century, there was a happier link with the Savile family, who with the Dukes of Newcastle, owned Wellow and were influential in Wellow history. When the Savile family sold their estate in 1938, many farmers and cottagers bought their properties.

Many of these properties have grazing rights on the common greens (about 40 acres). These were granted to householders, who lost grazing after the various Enclosure Acts. These rights are called tofts, and different animals represented so many tofts. The tofts had to be registered with the Government in 1968. The affairs of the toft owners are looked after by a committee, who meet regularly to see that the greens are mown and kept in a good state. The fishing rights of the dam are rented to a fishing club, and by courtesy of the lord of the manor, the committee use the income for maintenance purposes.

Since the 1950s many amenities have disappeared, apart from two pubs and the post office. In the past the village had a saddler, a cobbler, a blacksmith, a joiner-wheelwright, a butcher, a chairmaker, three grocery shops, five pubs and a school.

Planning is strictly controlled, so that the atmosphere of the village does not suffer by anything which would destroy the special area of the green and its surrounds. The newer part of the village is to the south on Eakring Road, and is practically a community of its own, with a warden and community centre to cater for the elderly of the area.

The church of St Swithin was erected about the time of Richard I, in 1189, and a major rebuilding programme took place in 1878. There are three bells dated 1560, 1660 and 1635. These bells are rung every 19th September, in gratitude for the deliverance of a Lady Walden, who visited the village over 200 years ago and became lost in the local woods. The sound of the bells guided her home and she left money for the bells to be forever rung on that date.

At the entrance to the village at the toll bar, are two large old houses, Wellow Hall and Wellow House. The Hall at one time was used for a period as a cottage hospital. Wellow House was the home of Lord Savile's estate agent in the 1800s. It is now used as a private educational trust school.

West Leake ❧

Approached along winding country roads, West Leake is a small village with one main street and a population of around 100 people. It is attractive, unspoilt and rural although within reach of Nottingham, Loughborough, East Midlands Airport and the M1 motorway.

The village name is recorded in the Domesday Survey (1086) as Leche, derived from the brook which flows through the village.

The village has two Roman tracks on its boundaries and there is evidence of Roman occupation in the area. Along the boundary of the brook stands a medieval moated manor site with its fishponds still in evidence. This was occupied by the lords of the manor from 1150 to 1750. There were two mills, one a windmill and the other a watermill

West Leake Village Hall

which was granted by King John in 1200. In later years the village consisted mainly of Elizabethan and Georgian farmsteads and farm labourers' cottages.

Today, the farms and farm buildings along with the cottages have been sold for private homes – gone are the thatched cottages and the village pump. The farmlands have been taken over by an agricultural consortium with the loss of many hedgerows, and many of the ancient footpaths have been diverted around the edges of the fields. The many ponds have been filled in. The main street is at times busy with traffic: gone are the days when cricket was played across the street. A few new houses have been built since 1950, but care is taken to maintain the character of the village.

The 12th century church that stands in the centre of the village is both a part of history and an active influence in society. The oldest part of the church has a small Norman window and a blocked up Norman door on the north side. It was enlarged in the 13th century and restored in 1878. It contains three interesting medieval monuments, including an effigy of Sir John Leek who is buried in the church. There is a more modern

178

window on the south side, depicting a view of the church and the local scene, well designed in delicate colours and with interesting detail, including a snail and a spider's cobweb.

The Mills family played an important part in the village. William Mills, born in 1780, started a basket making business: the osier beds were nearby. He worked entirely for the London trade and made letter trays for the Houses of Parliament. His sons and grandsons spread throughout the surrounding villages taking their trade with them. William's house, with its Tudor chimney, comprised a village inn, a basket making shop and a village oven, where the villagers took their bread and pies to be baked.

A village school was built in 1850 by Lord Belper (of neighbouring Kingston-on-Soar) who at that time owned the village. Children paid one penny per week to be educated. Until the Education Act of 1880 there was much absenteeism. Children stayed away to help their parents in the fields, some helping their mothers in the basket trade by buffing (peeling) the willows. At this time farm labourers' wages were low, ten shillings per week, and many had large families who lived only on bread and vegetables. In inclement weather a labourer would not be paid if he could not work. Lady Belper was concerned at the low standard of living of the children and she provided bread and cheese in the school. In the sewing lessons, it is recorded that Elizabeth and Sarah Mills' task was to make by hand the parson's shirts and nightshirts.

The school has now closed and is used as the village hall. A vigorous committee keeps the building in fine shape and it is widely used, regularly by the Women's Institute and the Young Farmers, and also for flower and vegetable shows, whist drives and other social occasions.

Weston 🌿

Weston, a tranquil, sleepy village where the pace of life meanders gently along the Old Great North Road. A likely location, you may think, to learn of a romantic but tragically sad legend.

The story takes place at a splendidly grand country farmhouse set in a magnificent canopy of greenery. This picturesque building was once the Black Lyon, a major coaching inn before the arrival of the Great Northern Railway.

The tale says that in the mid-18th century a footman by the name of John Morris took a sharp flint to a window and wrote an ode to express his feelings at being in competition for his loved one.

On the west facing window pane in the dusty old servants' quarters at the inn he inscribed:

> 'While this stone doth cut
> the most enduring glass
> why must there be two
> to share a pretty lass'.

In expressing his broken heart so poetically, he was late for the coach on which he was supposed to ride. As there was a steep penalty for missing a coach in those times he ran as fast as he possibly could to try to catch it. The legend says that he ran himself to death.

He was laid to rest in the grounds of the village's medieval rural church, dedicated to All Saints. The epitaph upon the stone reads:

> 'Here lieth the body of John Morris
> son of Charles Morris
> by Elizabeth his wife
> who departed this life
> February 17th 1749,
> in the 34th year of his age.

> I nimble footman once would out run death
> I ran too fast until I lost my breath
> Death overtook me and made me his slave
> And sent me with an errand to my grave.'

The house stands at the entrance into Weston, which is a warm and friendly village with hospitable people, and although the village is slowly growing it is still a close-knit community. Many of the villagers possess old rural skills in art and craft work.

Open fields surround the village, which gives a sense of space and never-ending countryside, and cattle and sheep graze on the pastures.

The village hall, the former village school, provides a centre for many activities for the young and old. It hosts the annual Harvest Supper and all other traditional events such as the annual church and village hall fairs.

Widmerpool ✍

Widmerpool is one of Nottinghamshire's oldest villages, believed to have been in existence in Roman times, and adjacent to the settlement at Vernemetum (Willoughby) on the Fosse.

It has always been an estate village, there being a 'Widmerpool' family as far back as 1283, including in 1333 a John de Widmerpool, who attended a Parliament in York. There were a number of disputes recorded during the reigns of Henrys IV, V and VI concerning ownership of village land, between the Cromwell, Pierrepont and Heriz families. Widmerpool then became embroiled in the Civil War, being near to the site of the battle of Willoughby Fields, and two soldiers are buried in the churchyard in unmarked graves. The wealthy Robertson family from Scotland entered village history in the early 1800s, at a time when the village, church and Elizabethan manor house were in a poor state of repair. They rebuilt every cottage in the village, and today there are a number of stone cottages and estate houses still existing. The Old School House, Gardener's Cottage, the Coach House, and Home Farm, believed to be the oldest house in the village, were all part of the estate.

The church was as neglected as the rest of the village, and to make matters worse in 1836 lightning struck the spire, demolished the roof and broke windows. With considerable help from the Robertsons (who had by then confusingly changed their name to Robinson) a new church was built (1888–96).

The Robinson family built the new Widmerpool Hall on higher land overlooking the village, and this remained the principal private house in Widmerpool, until the estate, having changed hands several times, was finally broken up in the 1950s. The Hall became the AA national training centre. The Hall's village association still exists, and from time to time the present owners allow the village the use of some of the beautifully maintained rooms. There is no longer a village hall, the building having been sold in 1975, and the proceeds invested in a charitable trust for the benefit of the inhabitants.

The village economy was until recent times almost entirely agricultural or connected with the estate, with a number of farms and smallholdings, a smithy and a large rectory. Nearly everyone was employed on the land or in the Hall as a farmworker, servant, groom, gardener, dairymaid, laundress, teacher or similar. The farms and smallholdings were eventually sold off, and today there are only five farms in the parish.

There is no longer a school, and there is no shop, public house or post office. There are still only about 60 households, so it is a small friendly place in which to live. Some older residents, who were tenants or servants of former owners of the Hall, have recorded their memories of days gone by: of Boxing Day parties for tenants with a present for every child; of WI canning sessions during the Second World War; of the vicar with the appalling stutter; of the evacuees who came and went (though one remains to this day working on a farm); of the early Barton Bus Service (the founder is buried in the churchyard); of Bonfire Night parties in the Paddock and Mrs Rimmer's treacle toffee.

Inevitably, the village has changed. However, in such a pleasant small rural community, everyone knows each other, the Quorn Hunt meets here sometimes, children can run into any house for help, and the old people are cared for.

Wilford 🍃

Wilford, mentioned in the Domesday Book, is still a very pleasant village on the banks of the river Trent, approximately one and a half miles from the centre of Nottingham. The name is said to be derived from a ford across the river and the name of the church, St Wilfrid's.

Wilford has expanded slowly since the 1950s, from a small farming community into quite a large area, spreading the boundaries of the original village to encompass several mini housing estates, Silverdale being the largest of these, but still retaining a village atmosphere at its heart.

St Wilfrid's, dating from the 14th and 15th centuries, is a thriving focal point to village activities and the community is very fortunate to have two church halls, both of which are used frequently throughout the week.

Benjamin Carter, a former rector of Wilford, founded the Church of England school in 1736, and in 1986 the school celebrated 250 years with many varied activities. This school is one of four in the village.

The main road runs from a bridge crossing the river Trent, originally built as a toll bridge in 1870 by Sir Robert Clifton, a local landowner, and the toll rights were retained by the Clifton family until 1969 when it was taken over by the local council. They in turn closed it to motorised traffic in 1974. The bridge was demolished and replaced with a new pedestrian and cycle bridge giving access to the centre of Nottingham – a walk of some 15 minutes. Before the toll bridge was built, people were brought across the river by a ferry, and today the Ferry Inn remains a lively hostelry and a reminder of days gone by.

Wilford has, through the ages, been a popular village to wander through, perhaps on a summer evening for a drink at the Ferry Inn or a Sunday afternoon stroll to enjoy the peaceful environs created by the river and village atmosphere.

To mention just one of the listed buildings, Wilford House was designed by Loughborough architect Samuel White in 1781, and was the home for many years of the Forman-Hardy family, who own and run the *Nottingham Evening Post*. William Wilberforce, who campaigned for the ending of slavery, stayed here whilst drawing up his Abolition Bill. The house has been very successfully restored and is now used as business premises.

Facilities in Wilford include two public houses, library, garden centre, car repair workshop, post office and general store, newsagent and general store, and a Co-op which has, since the 1960s, grown from a small wooden building to a mini supermarket.

Although Wilford has spread far beyond its original boundaries there is still the nucleus of a village atmosphere which draws in the new community to take part in rugby, cricket, bowls and even American football.

Although there are now no farms as such, Wilford still retains quite an area of green land and is fortunate in having two village greens. One of the local residents has a large herd of Nubian goats which are taken each evening to graze on the fields by the river. Another keeps a flock of doves and a flock of hens and provides many locals with fresh eggs, and several residents keep horses.

Even though so close to a busy city, the village has somehow managed to retain a tranquil and peaceful atmosphere which is much appreciated by all who live in Wilford.

Willoughby on the Wolds ✬

Willoughby on the Wolds, as the name suggests, nestles among the gentle hills of South Nottinghamshire, almost on the Leicestershire border. This proximity to another county often causes confusion with postal, telephone, water and electricity services. The origin of its name was a Danish word, Wilgebi, meaning village of the willows. Just outside the village by the side of the Fosse Way is the site of a Roman settlement, Vernemetum, and close by is the site of an Anglo-Saxon burial ground.

A minor battle of the Civil War was fought in a field near the church, where a Royalist officer is buried. It is reported that villagers climbed the church tower to watch the proceedings, and that the brook ran red with blood. The church is about 800 years old; it houses a 14th century chantry chapel, with sculpted figures of the Willoughby family. The village gave its name to the family of Wollaton Hall. Near the church is the school built by the Education Committee on church land in 1863. This led to a court case being held to decide who was responsible for the education of the children, the Church or the Education Committee. The Committee won the day.

At present there are about 400 inhabitants in the village. Seventy years ago it was a real agricultural community with 13 farms. Life centred around the church, Methodist, Baptist and Primitive Methodist chapels, the school, the public houses, the shop and the farms – today how different it is! There are only three full working farms, sadly no chapels and one public house. There is a shop which is now a mini-market, a baker and a pork butcher. The school has been threatened with closure three times, and each time the villagers have fought for it to stay open and won.

A frequent sight in the winter is the Quorn Hunt. It meets in Willoughby several times in the season, and in the villages nearby. To many, the familiar figure of Prince Charles has become a regular sight.

Mrs Wood is a well remembered character. She was an eccentric Roman Catholic lady who generally wore a long black cloak, and often walked to Nottingham (eight miles) to attend Mass, with peas in her shoes as a penance! She had her beautiful house pulled down because she thought the evil spirits were in it, and the rats wouldn't say their prayers!

The Second World War caused a small ripple in the calm of village life. Evacuees came from Nottingham, Birmingham and London. For a time the numbers in the school swelled and there was some excitement, then they went home and the village was as before. Gradually building was allowed again, new houses appeared. Mains water and main drainage came – great innovations, no more wells, pumps, and water carts!

Woodborough

Rising from the Dover Beck to 470 ft at Dorket Head and surrounded by unspoilt scenery, the long village Main Street extends along the valley floor and has the Woodborough Beck running through it. There was a settlement here from early times when it was known as Udeburg (Ude's fort) and in Fox Wood there is an oval Iron Age earthwork and hillfort with evidence of later Roman occupation.

From the 16th to the early 20th century the village was a framework knitting centre, as witnessed by many cottage windows and old knitters' workshops still in existence. As late as 1844 there were still 191 frames working but as this cottage industry gradually declined many of the knitters and their families turned to market gardening as the soil is very fertile.

A famous villager was the Rev George Brown, born in 1759 into a family of framework knitters. In 1788 he became an itinerant minister preaching the gospel as he travelled far and wide; he was known as 'the Walking Concordance' on account of his extensive knowledge of the Bible. He died in Woodborough in 1833 and is buried in the churchyard.

The church, dedicated to St Swithun, has a Norman font and north porch doorway. The tower was built in the 13th century with additions made in the 15th and the handsome 14th century chancel was erected by Richard de Strelley, Knight of the Shire who represented the county in Parliament from 1331–1336. There were four bells in the tower and a local rhyme describes their sound in comparison with neighbouring churches.

> Calverton crack pancheons
> Woodborough merry bells
> Oxton ding dongs
> Lowdham egg shells.

Woodborough Hall was built in the 17th century on the site of one of the former manors by Philip Lacock. It has a magnificent carved well staircase. Alterations carried out in 1850 for Mansfield Parkyns were probably the work of the famous local architect T. C. Hine.

The old vicarage on Lingwood Lane has a Pancake Bell tower and the bell is rung at 11 am every Shrove Tuesday to tell the housewives to prepare the batter for their pancakes. The original Woodborough Woods school was established in this building in 1736 and transferred to the 'Old School' in 1878 and to new premises in 1968, all within a stone's throw of one another. The village pinfold is still maintained on Main Street.

Woodborough Feast is celebrated on the first Sunday after the 2nd July and nowadays there are sports and a tea for the children, a special service on Feast Sunday and usually a small fair and steam engines. In times past the feast was held at sheep shearing time and took the form of a 'Fromety Feast' when villagers went to the Hall to celebrate with fromety (wheat)-cakes. Elizabeth Bainbridge was one of the Hall owners in the 18th century who maintained this tradition and was well known for her benevolence in many ways.

Plough Monday was another important date when local lads acted their version of the traditional mummers' play, going round the cottages by the light of a stable lantern to perform this ancient rite with the following words:

> In comes I, old Easom Squeesom,
> On my back I carry a besom,
> In my hand a frying pan,
> Don't you think I'm a jolly old man?
>
> In comes I, Big Belly Ben,
> Can eat more meat than ten score men.
> Eat a pig, eat a calf,
> Eat a butcher and a half.
> And then my big belly's not full.
>
> In comes I, the soldier.
> What can you do?
> I can shoot!
> Then shoot him! (shoots Big Belly Ben)
>
> In comes I, the Doctor!
> What can you do?
> I can cure hipsy, pipsy, palsy and gout,
> Pains within and pains without.
> Cure him then! (they point to Big Belly Ben)
> (Doctor kneels and cures him)

186

Then they sang 'We are the jolly ploughboys' and were given a glass of home made wine and continued on their merry rounds.

Other musical traditions were the village band which performed well into the 1950s and the Woodborough Carol was sung at Christmas and other special services. Sunday school parades used to take place on Easter Monday and Whit Monday.

At one time there were about a dozen alehouses in the village; some such as The Bugle Horn and the Half Moon have disappeared and others such as The Cock and Falcon, The New Inn, and The Punch Bowl have become private residences. The only two which remain are The Four Bells and The Nag's Head.

Today the village has doubled in size with modern housing developments, although most of Main Street and some other areas have been declared a conservation area. The population is still involved in mixed farming and market gardening but there is also a large commuter element. A large number of very active organisations cater for all age groups and interests.

Wysall 🌿

Wysall, entered as Wysoc in the Domesday Book, is a small village of some 300 inhabitants, situated ten miles south of Nottingham, close to the Leicestershire border. Interestingly, the number of inhabitants has remained fairly constant over the years. Even the First World War failed to deplete the numbers since all the menfolk involved survived – a handsome clock on the church tower provided by grateful villagers is a constant reminder of this. The village, despite recent building, still boasts two working farms and has retained a 'village' character, but many of the amenities associated with a corporate village life have disappeared.

In 1960 the lack of a car was no hardship. The village had a butcher's shop, a hairdressing salon, a garage, providing repairs to cycles, farm machinery and cars, and above all a village post office and general store, which sold everything and was essentially the focal point of the village. Two bakers delivered three times a week, and a fish lady and a green-grocer also called weekly. The village school built in 1871, was thriving and Guides and Brownie packs flourished. The WI, although member-ship was relatively small, was very active. Evening classes were held in the school in the evenings, and events such as the Harvest Supper and the Bonfire Party were lively social functions.

Sadly, today many of these amenities have disappeared. The school closed in 1971, the post office and shop closed in 1985. The hairdressing salon is no more, the butcher's closed in 1978 and no baker calls today. Although the village boasts a high proportion of children, approximately one third of the population, there are no Brownies or Guides or any organised activities for them. The WI no longer exists. Indeed, many of the older residents, often natives of the village, with no means of transport, are seriously disadvantaged. Admittedly a butcher, fish lady and a greengrocer still call once a week but for necessary services, such as the collection of a repeat prescription from the doctor (two and a half miles away), the postal services have to be used – additionally difficult without a post office! The postmaster from a neighbouring village attends the village hall once a week to pay out pensions and to sell stamps but this doesn't allow for a lapse of memory of a forgotten birthday, or any other such emergency between his visits!

Wysall, in its small way, is trying hard to retain a communal life; the village bought the former school to use as a village hall – various activities, fund raising, social and educational, are held there; annual events such as the Strawberry Fayre and the Harvest Supper still flourish.

Index